PROFIT FIRST FOR CONTRACTORS

ALSO BY SHAWN VAN DYKE

The Paperwork Punch List: 28 Days to Streamline Your Construction Business

PROFIT FIRST
FOR
CONTRACTORS

TRANSFORM YOUR CONSTRUCTION BUSINESS
FROM A CASH-EATING MONSTER
TO A MONEY-MAKING MACHINE

SHAWN VAN DYKE

Copyright © 2018 by Shawn Van Dyke

This publication is designed to provide accurate and authoritative information in regard to the subject matter covered. It is sold with the understanding that the publisher and author are not engaged in rendering legal, accounting, or other professional services. If you require legal advice or other expert assistance, you should seek the services of a competent professional.

While the author has made every effort to provide accurate telephone numbers, internet addresses, and other contact information at the time of publication, neither the publisher nor the author assumes any responsibility for errors or for changes that occur after publication. Further, the publisher does not have any control over and does not assume any responsibility for author or third-party web sites or their content.

All rights reserved.

ISBN: 9781790264506

For my wife, Katie. Thanks for encouraging me to go fishing.

CONTENTS

FOREWORD

1

INTRODUCTION

5

Chapter 1
THE CRAFTSMAN CYCLE

17

Chapter 2
MAKING CENTS - UNDERSTANDING THE FINANCIAL STATEMENTS

33

Chapter 3
THE BIGGEST PROBLEM FOR CONTRACTORS – THE DIFFERENCE BETWEEN MARKUP AND MARGIN

51

Chapter 4
HOW PROFIT FIRST FOR CONTRACTORS WORKS - SETTING UP YOUR ACCOUNTS

59

Chapter 5
BECOMING A PROFIT FIRST CONTRACTOR - INITIAL ASSESSMENT

71

Chapter 6
COMPARING APPLES TO APPLES

85

Chapter 7
FORGET INDUSTRY STANDARDS

97

Chapter 8
RIPPING OFF THE BAND-AID

115

Chapter 9
DESTROYING DEBT

149

Chapter 10
MEASURE YOUR METRICS

161

Chapter 11
GROUP COACHING

181

EPILOGUE

193

ACKNOWLEDGMENTS

197

Appendix 1
PFC GLOSSARY OF TERMS

201

Appendix 2
MARGIN & MARKUP TABLE

205

Appendix 3
PFC INITIAL ASSESSMENT FORM

207

Appendix 4
CLOSING RATE TABLES

209

FOREWORD

Martin is extraordinary at what he does. He builds decks, installs doors and can mount a perfectly level 150lb railroad tie as a fireplace mantel, by himself. I know it, because Martin is my contractor. We use him exclusively for the work on our house. There is just one problem. He struggles with profit.

It is a strange conundrum, since Martin is booked out three months in advance. He is in extreme demand. That fireplace mantel I mentioned, that was ours. My wife and I scoured the local area to find an old railroad tie that would complement our fireplace. Once we found the right piece, I immediately texted Martin and he got back to me quickly. He always does.

"Martin, we have a new mantel we want installed. Do you have any availability?", I texted.

"Hey Mike! Yes. I can install it on the first Saturday..." Martin responded.

The most important part of the communication was the three dots "..." They sat there ominously on my phone as Martin continued to type on his side. Then it came through.

"of November."

It was July.

Ugh. I would say my heart sank, but it is what I expected. Martin is in high demand. In fact, most contractors are. Many contractors have more work than they can handle. Yet there is a weird problem. Many contractors aren't profitable.

I was at the house when Martin arrived one week before Thanksgiving. As business has it, he was unable to arrive the first week in November due to unexpected scheduling conflicts. He fit me in when another project of his had an unexpected delay.

We chatted before Martin started drilling into the stone to mount the mantel. I asked him about his business, assuming things were wonderful. I mean, it is every entrepreneur's dream to have overwhelming demand, or so I thought.

"Not great," Martin responded to my question about how his business was going.

"What do you mean?" I asked.

Martin when on to explain that he was overwhelmed with work. He was spending twelve hours a day, every day, doing work and then another three to four hours a day trying to run the business - ordering supplies, scheduling jobs, billing clients, and collecting from those clients who seemed to always "lose the bill" that Martin sent.

He went on to explain that he was thinking about shutting down and working for someone else. The lack of money coupled with huge amounts of work was causing huge amounts of stress. He went on to share that if he didn't shut down soon, he would have more debt than he could ever afford.

In an exasperated breath he added "I didn't realize I needed an accounting degree to run my business. Where does all the money go?"

It is awkward that those exact words trigger a smile for me, as it did when Martin said it. The smile comes from the fact that Martin is only a few hours away from permanent profitability. He simply needs to know one simple rule: take your profit first.

I suspect that the reason you have this book right now is because you can relate to Martin's story. I wouldn't be surprised if you have more work than you can handle. I wouldn't be surprised if your clients love you and are (for the most part) willing to wait for you. And I wouldn't be surprised that even with all that good fortune, you still struggle with profit. I wouldn't be surprised, because that is the nature of the construction industry. Profit rarely happens.

But it does not need to be that way. Not even close.

It is shockingly easy for a contractor to achieve profitability. You don't need to work more and you surely don't need an accounting degree. You simply need to follow a simple system that allows you to operate your business like you always have, but channels the money you have to bring about permanent profitability. You in fact don't need to change at all, the system does.

The game changing system is right here, in your hands (or your earbuds). *Profit First for Contractors* will make you permanently profitable. I guarantee it. But you need to make a guarantee too. You need to commit to reading this entire book and implementing it every step of the way. You need to stick with the system even when it challenges your thinking. You need to take your profit first even when you feel you can't. You see, by taking your profit first your business will guide you (at times painfully) to distinguish what makes money and what doesn't, and you need to stick with it.

And I can't think of a person more qualified on this planet to teach you this system than Shawn Van Dyke. Shawn knows the construction industry. He knows the nuances and the unique needs. He knows what it is like and he knows, assuredly, how to make contractors permanently profitable. You see, Shawn doesn't just teach this... he lives it. Shawn was first his own Profit First client. Then he did it for countless other contractors. And now he is delivering it to you through this book.

I can argue that you likely just made the best investment in your life by getting this book. And I now ask that you take action and do what Shawn is about to teach you.

Funny enough as I am writing this (one week after Thanksgiving) I received two delightful calls. One was from my father, who said he loved the mantel at our house and how it "completed the home." The second call was from Martin.

"I did it Mike. I set up the accounts. I am doing the Profit First system. I am literally only ten days into it and I already have profit accumulating in my business. I don't know if this will continue to be this way next month or next year, but I feel confidence in my business again. I can see the light at the end of the tunnel. This is working."

"I don't think it will be this way next month or next year. I think it will be this way permanently," I responded. Time will tell, but if Martin sticks with the system, then the odds for permanent profitability are very much in his favor.

And, if you do what you are about to learn from Shawn, then the odds for permanent profitability are very much in your favor too.

- Mike Michalowicz

INTRODUCTION

Today I paid our quarterly taxes out of the tax account with ease because of Profit First. This was the first quarterly payment that we made without struggling to find the money that we owed to the IRS [and state]. And...there's money left over in the account. WHAT?!?

- Jayme Martin, Beautiful Chaos Renovations - April 10, 2018

"If I can't make this work, then I don't know what we are going to do."

Through the phone, I could feel the desperation and stress that my new client, Jayme, was under. He'd left his corporate job as the Global IT manager for a large corporation just a year before. He joined forces with his wife, Sarah, who had built a growing interior design business, and together they were Beautiful Chaos Renovations, a design and remodeling firm in Minneapolis, Minnesota.

By the time Jayme and I started working together, there was more chaos than beauty, and the strain the business was putting on Jayme and his family was reaching the breaking point. Jayme told me he could always go back to his corporate job making good money, but he wouldn't have a family life. He would have to sacrifice the life he and Sarah wanted for themselves and their children.

Jayme had chosen to prioritize quality of life over a big paycheck, but on this day, in this moment, the construction business was sucking the life out of him just like the corporate world did.

"Something has to change. I can't continue to live like this," Jayme said.

Jayme was caught in a vicious cycle. I call it the craftsman cycle, a cycle many construction business owners get sucked into. It's responsible for years of frustration, lost money, and damaged relationships. Construction business owners get so sick and tired of doing the same things, chasing work, working for the wrong clients, and not understanding the numbers, that they throw their hands up in desperation. They don't know what else to do. In an act of desperation, they sometimes reach out for help and when they reach out to me, they're drained, pissed off, lonely, and scared.

From a coaching perspective, the frustrated and desperate construction business owners like Jayme make the best clients. They are ready to take action. They need results, and they need them quickly.

Jayme had tried it his way for so long, but his way was not working. He was ready for change. He, like many other construction business owners, didn't realize he was trapped in the craftsman cycle. In fact, many construction business owners are not aware of this cycle. They burn out, go bankrupt, or continue to go round and round instead of moving forward. The craftsman cycle is the reason many construction companies never make a profit.

Are you stuck in the craftsman cycle? Look for these symptoms:

1. You're busy. You're booked for several months. You've been booked for several months, but you don't have any money.

2. You don't pay yourself a salary. And no, the sporadic owner's draws that your CPA told you to take don't count as a salary.

3. You don't understand the difference between markup and margin.

4. You are guessing at what your price should be instead of calculating your value.

5. You get most of the work you look at (a high closing rate), and you fear saying "no" to projects.

6. You tell yourself you are investing in your company when you can't pay yourself.

7. You don't know how to read your profit and loss statement.

8. You always seem to be behind schedule, and you have to start the next job before you finish the current one because cash is tight.

9. You believe there are industry standards for what you can charge, and you provide a lot of free work to your potential customers instead of selling your value.

10. Paying your taxes is a mystery and you depend on your CPA to tell you how much you owe.

If these symptoms sound familiar, you've picked up the right book.

Operating a construction business in the craftsman cycle leads to inefficiencies in production, working for free, and never making a sustainable profit.

Profit First for Contractors is the profoundly simple way to break the craftsman cycle. This system for managing the cash of your construction business is so effective that once I started teaching my clients Profit First, I had three clients call me in the first year and say practically the same thing: "Shawn, what am I supposed to do now? My business requires so much less of my time. I am making my margins, working for the right clients, and have the right people in place. What do I do next?"

My answer: "Whatever you want."

When you implement Profit First for Contractors, the doors are wide open. You can start another division within your current business. You can start another business or expand into a new location. You can hire the right people to run your business and just own the dang thing. You can even get back on the tools if that's what you want to do. You have the freedom to do what you want.

Throughout this book you will hear stories about construction business owners just like you, who broke out of the craftsman cycle and started running a business rather than just making a living. They started paying themselves a regular salary for the work they did within the business. They started charging the right price for their work, which produced the cash flow they needed to hire the right people. They stopped working for free and started saying no to the wrong clients. They were able to pay their taxes and make a profit to show for all the hard work they had done.

Why I Wrote this Book

I am on a mission to change the way the world views the trades. I believe the best way to accomplish my mission is to help construction business owners make a profit and build world-class companies.

I intend to elevate society's view of construction professionals from the unsophisticated "couldn't-do-anything-else-so-they-ended-up-in-the-trades" stereotype to what they truly are – business professionals who provide an extraordinary service through devotion to their craft, their customers, and their communities.

That's why when I read Mike Michalowicz's book, *Profit First*, I knew I had to bring his philosophy and the Profit First system to the construction industry.

But my relationship with Mike started years before I read *Profit First*. I was introduced to Mike through his first book, *The Toilet Paper Entrepreneur*. It was then our relationship began, unbeknownst to Mike, of course. Years later, I bumped into Mike again when I read his book, *The Pumpkin Plan*. After reading that book, I took the relationship up a notch. I considered Mike a mentor, although I had never met the man. Through reading *The Pumpkin Plan*, I discovered that Mike's thoughts on business and entrepreneurship mirrored my thoughts on running a successful construction business.

You could say that the *Toilet Paper Entrepreneur* was my introduction to Mike's business approach. *The Pumpkin Plan* was my courtship of his business philosophies, and then in the summer of 2017, I became married to his cash management system in *Profit First*.

I remember exactly where I was when I had the epiphany that would ultimately lead to me partnering with Mike and writing *Profit First for Contractors* (PFC for short). I was sitting poolside in Buffalo, WY while on vacation with my family, listening to the audio version of *Profit First*. I was about halfway through the book when I turned to my wife and revealed my epiphany, "This book is exactly what I have been teaching my clients, but it's packaged better. I am going to start teaching Profit First to my clients."

My wife replied, "That's great. Can you please get in the pool and keep our kids from drowning?"

The rest of the evening I couldn't stop thinking about how simple Profit First was, and the profound impact it would have on my clients' businesses.

As the sun started to go down, and pool time ended for the kids, I wanted to see if I could nab a few rainbow trout from the stream behind the hotel. I love to fly fish, and like any fly fisherman will tell you, we can't look at any body of water without thinking, "I wonder what they're biting on?"

I had already completed my dad-duty and helped my wife get the kids settled in for the evening, so I was free to grab my rod and net and splash around in the stream for a couple hours.

As I stood in the stream waiting for a trout to rise, I found myself thinking about how I could teach contractors the Profit First system in a way that would be specific to them. I wanted to translate Profit First into a language that would speak to contractors. Then it hit me. I was looking at the answer. Better yet, I was looking *through* the answer.

If you have ever been fishing, then you know how important polarized sunglasses can be to your fishing endeavors. Polarized sunglasses help reduce the glare from the sun that reflects off the water and enables you to see things below the surface of the water and in greater detail.

PFC is the polarized lens through which you should view the cash for your construction business. Profit First for Contractors, like Profit First, is a cash management system. It does not replace your accounting system. PFC is a filter, or a lens, that brings clarity and focus to your construction business.

Another way to put it is *Profit First* is like getting the right prescription glasses for your business, and PFC is like upgrading to polarized lenses. The PFC system allows you see the specific details of your construction business that are just under the surface, like those sometimes-frustrating rainbows.

Can you fly fish without polarized lenses? Sure. But why would you? It's easier to catch fish if you can see them and know where they are. The same philosophy applies to your construction business. Can you have a profitable construction business without implementing the Profit First for Contractors system? Sure. But it's a whole lot easier to manage your cash when you see where it's coming from and where it's going. Not being able to see below the surface of your construction business, beyond the financial reports, and how the money comes in and how it goes out, can put you out of business.

Most contractors go out of business in the first five years, and many who stay in business never make enough of a profit to grow a sustainable business. Construction business owners aren't paying themselves a regular salary because they don't know how to charge enough for their work. Many contractors believe they're only allowed to charge a 20% markup on their work, but they don't really understand how markup works in their businesses. They also confuse margin and markup, and it's this confusion and these assumptions that keep contractors from making a profit.

Profit First for Contractors will show you how to make the numbers work in your construction business and will give you a scalable and repeatable process to guarantee profits and manage your cash flow at the same time. Building upon the cash management methods described in *Profit First*, *Profit First for Contractors* will show construction business owners how to apply the general principles of *Profit First* specifically to a construction business. PFC will provide clarity about where the money is, where it's going, and how to use your money to build the business you have always dreamed of.

I am probably like you. I didn't go to business school. I have no formal education in business. At first, everything I learned about business came through trial and error. But, like you, I wasn't willing to give up. I was determined to make the numbers work. I had to. I had suffered through getting a couple of engineering degrees without math being one of my strengths. I knew I could figure it out. I just had to dig in and do the work. The livelihood of my family depended on it.

I realized that making money in construction is simple but not easy. In fact, very few things in life are simple and easy.

I started applying a numbers-based approach to running my construction business. I was going to let the numbers inform my decisions, and I was going to stop trying to guess my way to profitability and start calculating it. And that's exactly what I did. I learned the difference between markup and margin and used these two numbers to guide every decision in my construction business. This fact alone created the profit that I needed to sustain my construction business.

Years later, I had the opportunity to become the COO of a trim and millwork company. I used these same methods to grow that business. While there, I helped the business grow from eight field employees to twenty and the business went from losing money and being in debt to being out of debt and making a sustainable profit. This took eighteen months. I spent the next two-and-a-half years refining the operational and production systems, and when I left, that trim and millwork company was established as the premier service provider in our area.

Since then I have worked with construction business owners all over the world and taught them the same methods I present in this book. You will hear many of their stories and how *Profit First for Contractors* has transformed their businesses as well.

I am passionate about Profit First because it works, and it will transform the way you run your business.

When you use the systems outlined in this book, you will learn how to price your work to produce a profit, how to pay yourself for the value of the work you do within your own business, how to eliminate waste, and how to say "no" to clients that aren't willing to pay your price. You will work less and make more money doing it.

Remember Jayme from earlier? Something had to change and did it ever!

Jayme started implementing Profit First and immediately started to see the deficiencies in his general contracting business. He wasn't charging enough to make a profit, he was working for the wrong clients, and he wasn't charging for all the planning and design work he was doing.

After just six months of coaching and implementing Profit First for Contractors, Jayme was able to double his sales, pay his quarterly taxes on time, and make a profit for the first time in the history of the business. And as an added bonus, his family was able to go on vacation for a week, something they hadn't been able to do for a long time.

When was the last time you were able to take a vacation and pay for it in cash?

Jayme's results are incredible, but his story of success is not unique. Throughout this book you will meet other construction business owners who have had similar results. You'll meet business owners like Ken Alger, who owns K. Alger Woodworking and Custom Interiors - a custom millwork company in Rhode Island. Ken implemented Profit First within the first three months of starting his business and now fourteen years later, he attributes his success to the Profit First for Contractors system. No, Profit First didn't exist fourteen years ago, but the philosophy did. Some portion of every deposit you receive should be set aside, in separate accounts, for the various areas of operations of your business. Your grandparents or great grandparents might have used the envelope system in the same way to pay the bills. This money is for the mortgage. This money is for food, and this money is for fill-in-the-blank. If there isn't money in the envelope for that designated purpose, then we either have to go make some more or we have to cut back on something.

You'll hear from business owners like Kelly and Janice Stitzer, CIG Construction, from just outside Denver, Colorado. Kelly and Janice are a husband-and-wife team and run a dynamic roofing business. When we started implementing the Profit First for Contractors system, Janice was embarrassed to admit she hadn't reconciled their bank accounts for six months. Like many roofing contractors, the business is based on volume. But Janice quickly realized that increasing the volume of business didn't solve their money problems. After implementing Profit First for Contractors, CIG revamped their production systems and started charging properly for their work, identifying ideal clients and saying "no" to jobs and clients that were putting them out of business. Within ten months, they were able to completely transform their business and their bottom line.

And I want you to meet Zach Dettmore, a remodeling contractor in New Jersey. Profit First for Contractors ended Zach's slavery to his own business and transformed not only the way in which he operates his business, but also his mission. Zach explains, "I now see that I am not some sort of missionary trying to serve the greater good. I owe it to my family, my employees and myself to charge a fair price for quality work and my profits need to come first. If profits don't come first, I cannot do the work that I love."

In the pages of this book, you will discover how to make your construction business permanently profitable. In fact, I promise that if you follow the methods outlined in this book you will make a profit.

"C'mon Shawn. How can you make a promise like that?"

It's simple. After you read this book, you'll understand how this simple formula works:

Sales - Profit = Expenses

And why this profitless formula doesn't work:

Sales - Expenses = Profit

I promise that when you receive the next check from a client and you set the appropriate amount of profit in a separate bank account and you don't touch it, then at the end of the month, at the end of the quarter, and at the end of the year, that profit will still be there. When you practice this simple method month to month and quarter by quarter, then you will have profits for your business.

This is the simple part. But it will not be easy, at least not at first. Good habits are hard to start, and bad habits are hard to break. But the Profit First for Contractors system will simplify the process of making profits by reverse engineering your business operations and building profit into every aspect of your business.

Provided you follow the steps I recommend, you will have transformed your business by the end of Chapter 6. Do I want you to read the rest of the book? Absolutely. In fact, I insist on it because your work matters. Society isn't making carpenters, plumbers, electricians, masons, contractors, and other skilled workers any more. At least not at a rate that is filling the skilled labor gap.

Mike writes in *Profit First*, "Profit is not an event. Profit is a habit."

This book will guide you through how to break the old habit of guessing and hoping you'll eventually end up with a profitable construction business and transform the way you operate your business so that you can gain clarity about every aspect of your business.

Remember, Profit First is the prescription glasses business owners need to see their businesses clearly, and Profit First for Contractors is the polarized lens to see what is going on below the surface of your construction business.

I'm guessing you started your construction business because you love to build things and you were looking for some kind of freedom. Maybe you wanted the freedom that comes with making your own schedule or the freedom to produce work that met your high standards? Let's not forget about financial freedom. You started your construction business to make your bank account grow. That's why this book exists: to give you the financial freedom you want by transforming your cash-eating monster of a construction business to a money-making machine.

And we are going to do that starting today. There's no need to wait.

But we are going to tackle PFC the right way. Mike explains, "Your profit will start today and will occur permanently. All you need to do is commit to study this and then *do it*. Don't skip the doing. Pleeease do not skip the doing. You can't read this book, think 'awesome concept,' and go back to business as usual. You need to get off your butt."

As Jayme did, you need to draw a line in the sand and tell yourself, "I can't continue on like this. Something has to change." Profit First for Contractors is that change. Like Ken, you need to develop the discipline of viewing your income as specific stashes of cash that inform you how to operate the different parts of your business. Like the Stitzers, you need to stop focusing on volume and focus on value.

I want your construction business to be profitable. I want the profits from your construction business to give you your life back. I want you to spend less time worrying about the bank balance and more time focused on your family and the other things in your life that matter. I want you to show not only your friends and family, but also the world around you that choosing to be in the construction industry is one of the most rewarding and fulfilling careers available to this generation and generations to come.

Wow! I'm fired up. I hope you are. Let's do this thing. Let's make your construction business permanently profitable starting today.

Chapter 1

THE CRAFTSMAN CYCLE

The definition of insanity is doing the same thing but expecting a different outcome.

In the movie, *Groundhog Day* starring Bill Murray, weatherman Phil Connors finds himself forced to relive the same day over and over again. No matter what he does, he can't escape Groundhog Day.

Connors discovers he is trapped in February 2nd. Connors wakes up every day, to the same day. The same pattern. The same events. He is stuck in time. Nothing changes. Nothing advances. And he stays stuck until he learns the lesson he is meant to discover.

Have you ever felt that way? Perhaps you feel that way now. Do you feel stuck in the same pattern day in and day out? Does nothing advance?

May I be so bold as to suggest that, if you are stuck, you are, in fact, trapped in the craftsman cycle and need to learn. You need to learn the method to permanent profitability.

Phil Connors learns how to serve others and starts to become a better person. This new approach to life pays off, and he finally escapes his imprisonment in Groundhog Day.[1]

When you woke up this morning, did you feel like you were reliving your own Groundhog Day? Up early in an attempt to get ahead of the tasks that had to get done today before the phone started ringing with all the fires you had to put out? Then there was the actual work that had to be done. Perhaps it is a

---

[1] Shmoop Editorial Team. (2008, November 11). Groundhog Day Plot Summary. Retrieved September 5, 2018, from https://www.shmoop.com/groundhog-day/summary.html

combination of client meetings, production work, sales calls, answering other people's questions, and paperwork. Dear Lord, the paperwork. And before you know it, it's 2:30 pm. You haven't eaten lunch. You're starving. You can't think straight. You still haven't been able to get to that one thing that you had hoped to do, and time is running out. So, you kick the production in high gear. You push through the afternoon with intensity and before you know it, it's 5:30 pm. There's no way you're going to be home in time for dinner with the family. On the race home, you're getting in the last few calls to your employees, subs, or vendors in an attempt to salvage some level of productivity for the day. You pull in the driveway and sit in your truck and check off a few more boxes. Your significant other wonders what you're doing out there. It's now 7pm and you're exhausted. The day didn't go as planned, and you still have paperwork to do, bills to pay, and estimates to get out the door. You're exhausted and can't think straight, so you collapse in bed. As you lie there, your mind is racing thinking about what you weren't able to get done today and how you need to get up early tomorrow and get caught up before you head out in the morning. And the cycle repeats.

You, my friend, are caught in what I call the craftsman cycle - the seemingly never-ending loop of urgent tasks and responsibilities that keep you from gaining traction toward your important goals. Authors Chris McChesney and Sean Covey, in their book *The 4 Disciplines of Execution*, describe this cycle as being caught-up in the "whirlwind of the urgent." This whirlwind devours all the time and energy you needed to invest in planning your strategy for tomorrow and developing the systems for the future of the business.

Many construction business owners do not have systems. They are the systems. If the owner stops working, then the business stops. Period. No one sets out to create a Groundhog Day business. But that's what desperation does to you over time. You get caught in a cycle, and it can be difficult to break.

So, what's the solution? How do you not only break out of this cycle, but also build an actual business, one that serves you and provides for you without requiring you to do all the work? The solution is quite simple, and it begins by working with your natural tendencies, not against them.

Robbing Peter to Pay Paul and Patrick

I am sure you are familiar with the phrase "rob Peter to pay Paul." There is much debate about the origin of this idiom. According to Wiktionary, the phrase refers: "to times before the Reformation when Church taxes had to be paid to St. Paul's church in London and to St. Peter's church in Rome; originally it referred to neglecting the Peter tax in order to have money to pay the Paul tax".[2] Whether this explanation is historically accurate or not, we all know what the expression means: You are incurring a new debt to pay for a previous one. You use the money from one project to pay for the expenses of the next one.

When we use the money from Peter's project to fund the start of Paul's project, then we are constantly checking the bank account to see if there's enough money available, which creates what Mike describes in *Profit First* as "bank balance accounting."

This is how bank balance accounting works.

You look at your bank balance and see how much money is in there. When you started, anything above zero was a good day. But as more work lined up, then the bank account started to grow. This was a great feeling. You'd never seen so much money in your account before. But then the bills started to roll in and that balance started to dwindle. After a few weeks or months of this you started to develop a new "zero balance."

When you started, zero meant zero. But that was probably ok. Your business was just some side work or a just a series of small projects that you were doing to get started. You'd complete a project and maybe there was some money in the bank account. You thought that meant you made a profit, so you felt pretty good about your new venture. But that would only last a few days. That vendor invoice that you forgot to pay would surface, and the profit you thought you made was eliminated. After you paid that bill, then you realize that having $5,000 in your bank account was the same as having zero, because you knew there were expenses floating around out there that were going to surface any day.

---

[2] Rob Peter to pay Paul. (n.d.). Retrieved September 5, 2018, from https://en.wiktionary.org/wiki/rob_Peter_to_pay_Paul

As time goes on, and you continue to work for Peter and Paul, you are constantly checking the bank account. Your zero balance gets bigger and bigger. After months or years working like this, your zero balance could be tens of thousands of dollars.

A bank balance you once would have celebrated, let's say $20,000 in the account, now creates stress because you know you have payroll to meet next week, an insurance premium is due, and you purchased materials for the last job on your credit card. You see $20,000 in the account but you know that will evaporate within a week. In your mind, $20,000 is the same as $0.

Panic sets in. So, what do we do? We go find another Peter...we'll call him Patrick, so we can keep track of things. Patrick is hard-headed and cheap. He doesn't want to pay your price for the scope of work and demands to see line item pricing for his project to ensure he is not getting ripped off.

You know that $20,000 is quickly evaporating with each day that goes by, so you drop your price, provide Patrick with the line item pricing he demanded, and agree to take a 10% deposit instead of the 30% you typically require to pay for materials.

Now Patrick, who said he was ready to get started, doesn't return your phone call, doesn't respond to your email, and you wonder if you're going to get the job. You need that deposit, because seconds after Patrick said he was ready to go, you sent checks to a couple vendors, and submitted your payroll.

Your bank balance is now below your zero balance. You are on life support. The amount of cash left in the bank won't cover the materials you have to purchase for Patrick's job, even when you combine that with the 10% deposit you agreed to accept to start the job.

What can you do? You need cash now and time has run out. You then get a call from Paul. He needs a small job, not necessarily the type of job you like to do or would normally take, but you need cash. You tell Paul that you can start tomorrow and offer to do the job for cash or time and materials. A sense of relief comes over you because you will have some income in the next week, so you make a commitment to Paul.

And then it happens. Patrick calls back and says he's ready to go. You are now over committed, but the lure of that 10% deposit will help get you back above the zero balance, at least for a few days.

This is a painful process to describe, not only because this bank balance accounting is a brutal way to operate your business, but also because it brings up bad memories. I did the same thing, and as I write this I can remember those early mornings staring at the computer screen trying to figure out what my financial statements meant. But I would always return to the easiest thing to understand - my bank balance. That told the real story. I knew that was the money I had at that moment.

If this describes you, then congratulations. You are completely normal. This is how many construction business owners operate. They try to stay above the zero balance. It's human nature to look at what we have right now and make decisions based on that information.

It's a construction professional's nature to focus on the work. Building stuff with your hands is what gives you satisfaction. Managing the money is a stressor and drains your energy. So, when the money comes in and gets us above the zero balance we go back to the thing that gives us pleasure - work.

But the work - at least the way we have created it - is the problem. The work doesn't produce the income we need to operate a profitable business. Selling more of this work just expands the money problems. Mike explains in *Profit First*, "[T]he cycle starts all over again. If you haven't relied on it from the start, eventually the only 'solution' is to take on debt…"

Up to this point you have been telling yourself that your credit cards aren't *really* debt; they are just a way to finance operations, and you promise yourself to pay off the balance each month. But when Peter is a little past due on invoices for work completed and Paul decides that you took too long to do that thing "he could have done himself in less time" and doesn't pay the entire invoice, and Patrick doesn't send the deposit check, then you are in trouble. You open that line of credit, get another credit card, and just flat out ignore your lumber supplier's invoice.

This is how construction business owners end up getting stuck robbing Peter to pay Paul (and Patrick, too) and surviving from project to project.

This is no way to operate a business. This is no way to live. Let me ask you, did you start your construction business so that your mood and outlook on life would be determined by the daily balance of your bank account? I didn't think so. But that's exactly what we do. Bank balance accounting is human nature. We all do it. But this method of managing your business will never lead to success. It will never get you out of debt. You need to change. But change is hard. That's why you need something simple.

You need a simple method for managing your cash and operating your construction business that leverages our natural tendencies, rather than working against them. Mike explains in *Profit First*, "Without an effective money management system that does not require massive mind-set change, we get stuck in trying to sell our way out of our struggles."

We focus on selling more Peters and closing more Pauls and looking for more Patricks - just sell, sell, sell. But we can't sell our way out of a broken system. Selling more work at the wrong price for the wrong clients sucks us into a brutal cycle - the craftsman cycle.

Starting the Craftsman Cycle

Have you ever wondered how you got here? You have work booked several months out. In fact, it's more work than you've ever had backlogged before. That gives you a sense of security, but there's still an uneasy feeling in your gut. You don't understand how you could have been so covered up with work and for so long, but there's no money to show for it. You haven't paid yourself a regular salary in months, if ever, and you just gave in and pulled out some money to pay a few personal bills. How can you be so busy, doing such high-quality work, but have no money to show for it? It's a mystery.

Nope. It's the craftsman cycle, and you're trapped in it. In fact, you didn't even realize you were entering into it the first time you priced a job, but that's when it started. The cycle slowly expands over time, sucks you in, and disguises itself as many other things.

But make no mistake. It's a cycle and it's tough to break when you're in it because you can't see another way.

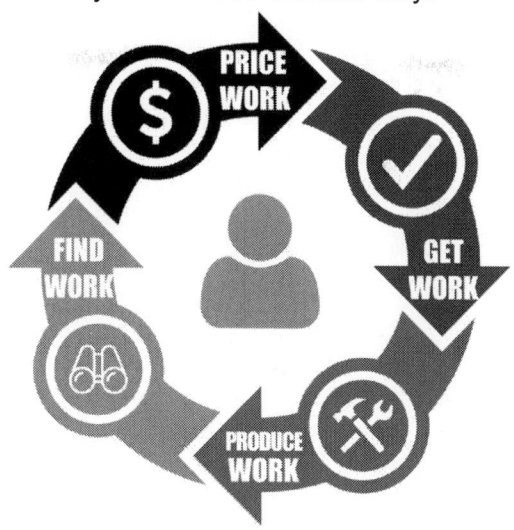

Figure 1. The Craftsman Cycle

If you're like many construction business owners, this is how the cycle works.

One day you looked up from your tool belt and realized you had some skills. In fact, you knew that the quality of your work was superior to the other people you worked with. This realization gave you confidence to start doing a few side jobs for friends and family. You were excited to be doing new stuff and getting your name out there and being your own boss, even if it was only for a few nights a week or on the weekends. But the extra cash in your pocket was nice and it was easier than you thought to make a dollar. You realized you could get work, and you were excited.

Then your reputation grew beyond your friends and family. People wanted what you had to offer, and you had to start estimating and selling your work to complete strangers. You didn't know what to charge, but you knew what your employer paid you and you figured you could give yourself a bit of a raise. So, you priced work based on your current wage plus some. You started getting busy. Every evening there was either another potential customer to see or there was work in progress. And weekends? There were no more weekends. You worked every weekend because you could really make some progress on your side hustle.

The work started piling up and gave you the confidence to take the leap and go out on your own. You did it!

It was an exciting and scary time. It was all on the line and you wanted work, so you priced every job that came in. You got so busy pricing work and getting work and producing work that months flew by. Money was coming in and money was going out, and the money was more than you'd ever seen before. You tried to learn what you could about the business side of things, but that was confusing and boring compared to producing the work.

You learned a lot during this time. Producing the work took longer than you thought, and the money didn't seem to match the effort that it required. You weren't sure where all the money was going, so you started checking the bank account every day. You noticed that not much money stayed in the business. Sure, there was a lot coming in, but there was a lot going out as well.

The bills started piling up because you couldn't produce the work fast enough. You decided to expand. You hired an employee or subcontracted some work. And that's when it happened. The money disappeared. Hiring an employee meant that you now had to manage someone else besides yourself.

This management took more of your time, which meant there was less time to produce work. When you weren't producing work, you weren't producing income. Having an employee or subcontractors got expensive. Although the balance in the bank account was higher than ever before, you knew that it would quickly go away because you had payroll and accounts payable that were due within a couple weeks.

So, you priced more work. Any work. Some work you would get, and some you wouldn't. The work you did get came at the cost of a lot of wasted time, negotiating and guessing. All this guesswork led to stress, and you started missing deadlines and putting clients off. But you couldn't put clients off too long. New clients and new projects meant new deposits and an influx of cash. You needed this cash to keep the lights on. But you were barely surviving. After several months or years of late nights and early mornings, you decided that you had to raise your prices. The math just wasn't working out. So, you did. You raised your prices.

And then it started to happen. You started hearing a word that you hadn't heard before. Your potential clients started saying "No." You found yourself under even more stress. So, you dropped your prices in order to get work and the cycle repeated itself.

The whole time this was going on, you kept checking the bank balance to see what you could afford to pay for that week. *Can I take some money out to pay myself? Which of my vendors are going to get paid this week?* But you have to pay your employees and subs, or they won't show up for work the next day.

This cycle of price work, get work, produce work, find work is the craftsman cycle, and it's a trap.

Operating a business in the craftsman cycle causes stress because it keeps you busy and never allows you to be focused. The only thing you focus on is work. You never have the time to focus on the business. There is a difference, a big difference.

The craftsman cycle gives us a false sense of security. We think that because we are busy, and money is coming in that we are making a profit. But there is a difference between revenue and profits. The craftsman cycle doesn't distinguish between the two. If you are focused on pricing, getting, producing and finding work, then you will inevitably generate revenue. But if that revenue isn't high enough to generate a profit, then you will inevitably run out of cash. Many construction business owners trapped in the craftsman cycle are actually going out of business with every job they take. Each project puts them a little further out of business. And it only takes one slip-up to bring this house of cards crashing down.

This was the case with Jason Mollak of JPM Construction, a specialty trim contractor in Omaha, Nebraska. When I first spoke with Jason, he was tens of thousands of dollars in debt, had floated his business on credit, and was taking any job he could to keep the money coming in. And then it happened.

A general contractor that Jason and his team were working for stopped paying Jason's invoices. After repeated requests for payment from Jason and promises from the general contractor that the checks were in the mail, the general contractor finally admitted that he couldn't pay Jason. He didn't have the money. Jason didn't know what to do. He not only needed a plan to get out of this mess but also a plan to keep it from ever happening again.

We developed a plan to get the money he was owed, but most importantly we developed a plan to make sure he could avoid this problem in the future. Jason went directly to the owner of the project and informed him of the situation and was able to get the money he was owed. That solved the immediate problem, but then he had to solve the bigger problem - breaking out of the craftsman cycle.

Sometimes clients are late in making payments. If this describes your clients, then the primary fix is to get better clients. But secondary to that solution is to build up cash reserves.

That's what Jason did by implementing Profit First for Contractors.

Through hard work and setting money aside for the contingencies that are inevitable in business, Jason was able to not only knock out his debt in six months, but also fundamentally change the way he operated his business. He explains, "By implementing Profit First, I could see where the money was going and how much we could spend on paying off the debts." And Jason elaborated about the best part: "We now have money in the bank and I am able to take my wife on a vacation (without our five girls) for the first time in eleven years. Not only were we able to accomplish that goal, but now my wife can see and feel the changes in the business. That is a huge accomplishment for me."

Jason was able to break out of the craftsman cycle, that day-to-day grind, and build a legacy for his family and his employees. The craftsman cycle is like a real-life Groundhog Day - the same thing over and over again without relief.

Profitability in your construction business depends on selling your work for the right price to the right clients in a way that generates a profit and positive cash flow for each project. If you don't have a system that produces profits and positive cash flow for your construction business, then you will operate in constant crisis. You can't focus on the right things when you are operating out of constant crisis and constantly checking the bank balance.

When you focus on the amount of money in the bank, you focus on the top line. "I need more money, now! How can I get more money now? I need to get more work." Top-line focus doesn't answer the real question, "Where does the money go?" In order to answer this question, you have to understand some basic financial principles and key financial reports.

If you search for the answer to your financial questions you will discover an accounting system called GAAP (Generally Accepted Accounting Principles) and financial reports like the income statement, the cash flow statement, and the balance sheet (see Chapter 2 for a further breakdown of these reports).

The problem with GAAP is that it is a way to analyze the finances within your business, but not a system to operate your business. GAAP is complicated and that's why it takes a CPA years of specialized training to develop the skills necessary to accurately organize this information for a business.

GAAP uses this basic formula to account for the earnings and expenditures of any business:

Sales - Expenses = Profit.

Allow Mike to explain: "Logically, GAAP makes complete sense. It suggests that we sell as much as we can, spend as little as we can and pocket the difference. But humans aren't logical...Just because GAAP makes logical sense doesn't mean it makes 'human sense.'" GAAP is the underlying force that fuels the craftsman cycle and makes us think that more work (sales) is the key to growth (profit).

This top line (revenue or sales) approach to operating a construction business hampers our ability to see what is happening within our business - specifically the expenses that accompany the top line. Yeah, we know we have some expenses, but as long as we sell more than we spend then we will make some money. But analyzing expenses is hard and takes time. Plus, if we don't know, then we can claim ignorance.

Ignorance is bliss. This was undoubtedly first said by a contractor who didn't want to know how much money he was spending on tools.

As the craftsman cycle continues, it usually gets bigger. It takes more jobs, more employees, and more expenses to service Peter and sell to Paul. Remember those guys?

Profit First Basics

> Mike describes the three fundamental flaws of GAAP in Profit First:
> 1. [I]t goes against human nature. No matter how much income we generate, we will always find a way to spend it - all of it. We can justify anything. GAAP is logical. Humans are not.
> 2. [It] teaches us to focus on sales and expenses first.
> 3. You need an accountant to get it right.

Here's how I summarize these three flaws, along with another I add to Mike's list:
1. Humans make purchasing decisions based on emotions rather than logic. We spend money and then justify that expenditure as necessary. Humans are really good at that. Our brains are wired that way.
2. We want what we want. We want more sales. When we sell more, then we "need" more stuff. We justify our needs by telling ourselves that we are "investing" in our business. This makes us feel (emotional response) better for not paying ourselves a salary or making a profit. GAAP makes us lie.
3. It is complex. Ask your CPA to explain how GAAP makes you money in a construction business, and you're likely to get an answer that might as well be in a foreign language. Plus, GAAP is open to interpretation.
4. It is a system to analyze your business as a whole, not a system to manage your cash. *Profit First* states, "Cash is the lifeblood of your business." If you don't have cash, you are out of business, even if the GAAP reports show you have made a profit. If you have cash, then you can survive another day.

To successfully run a profitable construction business, you need a super-simple system to manage your cash, one that you can understand without the help of an accountant. Mike writes:

> We need a system that can instantly tell us the truth about the health of our businesses, one that we can look at and know instantly what we need to do to get healthy; a system that tells us what we can actually spend and what needs to be reserved; a system that doesn't require us to change, but automatically works with our natural behaviors. Profit First is that system.

If Profit First is the lens through which you need to view your business, then Profit First for Contractors is the polarized lens that will allow you to see what is going on below the surface.

When Phil Connors, Bill Murray's character in Groundhog Day, learned to become a better person he regained his freedom. You need that same breakthrough - freedom from the craftsman cycle. You can have your happy ever after too. Whether you are just starting your construction business, or you have been in business for decades, you can transform your cash-eating monster to a money-making machine.

You can break the craftsman cycle. You just have to learn how to control and direct your actions to produce the results that you want.

It worked for Jason, and it will work for you, too.

What you will learn in this book is the key to taking control of your construction business and making it profitable, while paying yourself a salary and your taxes at the same time. Once you learn to apply this system, you never have to go back to being trapped in the craftsman cycle. Mike explains it this way: "You never have to exist off the leftovers again. You get to eat first. There's one way to fix your business - face your financials. You can't ignore them."

Ignorance is not bliss. It is death. Once you see beneath the surface of your company, you will be able to direct your accountant and educate her on how you make money in your construction business instead of being held hostage to what she says. You will be able take charge of your numbers and understand exactly what you need to do to build profits in your construction business. It will happen faster than you think. In fact, you'll be able to implement the Profit First for Contractors system within just a few more chapters. Keep reading.

Take Action Now

At the end of each chapter, I list a few actions steps that will move you through the journey of transforming your construction business from a cash-eating monster to a money-making machine.

This is where the rubber meets the road. Don't skip the doing part. Doing is the only way to break out of the craftsman cycle.

Some chapters have more action steps than others, but overall the action steps are small goals to achieve before moving on to the next chapter.

If you're like me, you enjoy checking things off your list. Reading this book all the way through gives you that sense of accomplishment. I get that. But if you read (or listen) to this book all the way through without stopping, promise me you will go back to each chapter and complete each action step.

Promise?

Action Steps

1. Draw a mental line in the sand and get some accountability. Go to www.profitfirstcontractor.com right now and download the pdfs on that page. These resources will help develop your Profit First for Contractors (PFC) system as you work your way through the rest of the book. Seriously. Go check it out. I am not going anywhere.

2. Set up your profit account with your bank and allocate 1% of your revenue going forward. I understand you may be skeptical and your understanding of the PFC system may be woefully insufficient at this point. But this step is so simple and so small, and the impact can be so massive, that I just ask that you do it now. Like right now. Yes...now. I'll wait.

Now that you've done that, send me an email (my email is Shawn@ProfitFirstContractor.com) with the subject line "I want to break the cycle" and tell me that you are committed to making your construction business permanently profitable. Email me now and make the commitment. Tell me a little bit about your business and why you are reading this book. I read all my emails and I will respond. I promise. I will send you a response. It may take me some time, but I will get back to you. This is my promise to you if you will make a commitment to me.

Let's do this.

Chapter 2

MAKING CENTS - UNDERSTANDING THE FINANCIAL STATEMENTS

"On paper everything looked great. The profit and loss statement showed a decent net profit, but wait, that money is not in the bank! Where did all that money go?"

- Janice Stitzer, CIG Construction

Have you seen the movie *The Sixth Sense*? If not, then you may want to skip this section because I am going to spoil the movie for you. And yes, I know the movie came out in 1999, so if you're under 30, you may have no idea what I'm talking about. You may need to skip this section, too.

Seriously, SPOILER ALERT to follow.

In my opinion, *The Sixth Sense* is a movie that can only be truly experienced once. Like most M. Night Shyamalan movies, the viewer spends most of her time wondering where this story is going and then BAM! - a huge reveal that you never saw coming. That revelation makes everything preceding it make sense.

That's exactly what happens to everyone the first time they watch *The Sixth Sense*.

SPOILER ALERT! (Don't say I didn't warn you.)

The climax of the movie happens when the audience realizes that Bruce Willis' character is dead and has been dead for most of the story.

If you're like me, this made for an enjoyable movie experience, and I spent the next couple of days wondering if I could have figured out that Willis' character died at the beginning of the movie.

As smart as I like to think I am, I have to admit that Shyamalan got me. I'm guessing he got you, too, unless you're one of those folks who says, "Naw, I figured it out." In that case, I would say you are a liar. Wink, wink.

The thing I don't like about *The Sixth Sense* is that I couldn't fully experience the movie a second time. The big thing had been revealed. I couldn't un-know what I knew. Watching it a second time, I did enjoy seeing how all the pieces of the story were woven together to create that initial "wow" moment. But I didn't experience the "wow" the second time like I did the first. I knew what I knew.

You're going to experience that same feeling after reading this chapter and doing the action steps. Your financial statements will no longer be a mystery to you. You won't be able to look at them and say, "I wonder where all the money is going."

It's fun to watch a movie and get sucked into the mystery of what's going to happen, but your construction business is not some Hollywood production with special effects and a perfectly choreographed ending. Your construction business is your livelihood, and the financial statements shouldn't be a mystery.

In this chapter, you are going to learn the math of your construction business. And it's not complicated like calculus or trigonometry. The math of your construction business is mainly addition and subtraction with a little algebra mixed in. At worst, we are going to do some high school level math.

The good news is that it's just math. Once you learn how this math works for your construction business, you will never need to learn it again. The math doesn't change. Everything else in your business will. Market conditions change. Trends change. Building science and materials are constantly evolving. And employees. Oh man, employees will change your business.

But math, that math isn't going to change. Math always stays the same. You just have to keep applying it in the same way to profitably operate your construction business.

Defining Profit First Terms

Note: In the next few chapters, I am going to introduce you to several accounting, *Profit First*, and *Profit First for Contractors* (PFC) terms. These terms have specific meanings, and you must understand what each one means in the context of this book. I have provided a Glossary of Terms in the Appendix of this book. You will want to refer to this Glossary of Terms often until PFC becomes like a second language for you. I have also provided a pdf of this Glossary of Terms at www.profitfirstcontractor.com. Download it and keep it with you while you are working through PFC. Also, the first time one of these terms is used in this book, I will capitalize the entire word, so you know the definition can be found in the Glossary.

With that said, let's start off with the most important equation you need to know for your construction business:

PRICE = COSTS x MARKUP FACTOR

The PRICE of any of your projects is the sum of the COSTS of that project multiplied by the MARKUP FACTOR (or simply MARKUP). The MARKUP needs to be high enough to pay for your EXPENSES and leave you with a NET PROFIT.

Before we move on, let's define a few more terms that we are going to be using in the rest of this chapter and throughout this book.

COSTS for a construction business are also referred to as COST OF GOODS SOLD (or COGS).

COGS for a construction business are typically the costs of the LABOR, MATERIALS, SUBCONTRACTORS, and EQUIPMENT. These are the things that you buy, mark up, and sell to your customers. (I am painting with a pretty broad brush here, but most of your COGS will fall into one of these general categories.)

If it's not a COGS, then it is an EXPENSE.

What's the difference between a COGS and an expense for your construction business? Here's a super-simple way to determine if something is a COGS or an expense: If you buy it, mark it up and sell it to your customer and it gets left out in the field, then it's probably a COGS.

For example: You buy materials, let's say some 2x4s. You mark them up and sell them to you customers. Materials are a COGS. Same thing applies to field labor. You "buy" labor from your field employees, mark it up and sell it to your customers. Labor is a COGS. These things (or the result or use of these things), along with subcontractors and equipment gets left out on the field.

What about your cell phone? You don't sell cell phones, but you certainly need a cell phone to operate your business. Since you don't buy, mark up, and sell cell phones, then the money you spend on your cell phone is an EXPENSE. Another example is food. You don't buy, mark up and sell food to your customers, but you probably spend money on business lunches or other meals to generate business. Food (meals and entertainment) is an expense.

So, the things you buy, mark up, and sell to your customers to generate an income for your business are your COGS.

Everything else is an expense.

Now let's define MARKUP. The markup is the amount of money that you add to your COGS to determine your PRICE. The markup is often expressed as a percentage. For example:

Let's say that you estimated your COGS to be $100 and you want to add a 50% markup to calculate your price. You would multiply $100 by 50% and add the product of that formula to your COGS. Your price would be $150.

Step 1. $100 x 0.50 = $50
Step 2. $50 + $100 = $150

This is how you would use a markup to determine your price.

But we can eliminate a step if we use a MARKUP FACTOR. Instead of multiplying the COGS by the MARKUP and then adding that number back to the COGS (a two-step process) we can multiply the COGS by the markup factor and get the same result in one step. For example:

Using the same numbers as above our COGS are $100 and our markup is 50%. Using the markup factor all we have to do is multiple the COGS by "1 + MARKUP" to get the same answer.

Step 1. $100 x 1.5 = $150

There is no Step 2.

I know this seems elementary but defining these terms and being absolutely clear on how we use them is vital to understanding how the numbers work as we proceed.

Now that we are clear that the markup is the amount (expressed as a percentage) that we add to the COGS to get the price, and the markup factor is just "1 + MARKUP", we should be on the same page when we use these terms going forward.

Net profit is the money that remains after the COGS and expenses are deducted. *Warning*: the previous statement is according to GAAP. We are going to approach net profit from a different perspective in the following chapters, but for now you need to understand the technical definition, so let's leave it at that.

The equation for NET PROFIT is:

NET PROFIT = INCOME - COGS - EXPENSES

The final term we need to define is INCOME. Again, I know this may seem silly, but we need to define this term, so we are on the same page. INCOME is equal to REVENUE. The total income for your construction business is also called TOP LINE REVENUE or GROSS REVENUE. Therefore, the terms income and revenue are interchangeable.

These terms are also interchangeable with the word price. The price of a project is the income you will receive when you perform the work. The income you receive for performing work is also called the revenue.

Therefore:

INCOME = REVENUE = PRICE

With these terms defined, we can start to understand the financial reports of your construction business. The first report we are going to break down is the income statement.

The Income Statement

The income statement is also known as the profit and loss statement (or P&L for short). These terms are also interchangeable. I know. It seems confusing. That's why we are taking it one step at a time.

The P&L is a summary of the revenues (income), costs (COGS), expenses, and resulting net profit incurred by the business during a given period of time.

For example, you can run your P&L for the last calendar year, the most recent quarter, or any period of time in which you want to see what the business did during that defined period of time. The P&L always has a beginning and an end.

There are four main areas of the P&L that give us the information we need to determine how the business has performed.

These four areas are:

1. INCOME
2. COGS
3. EXPENSES
4. NET PROFIT

The figure below shows how a typical P&L should look for a construction business:

MAKING CENTS – UNDERSTANDING THE FINANCIAL STATEMENTS 39

INCOME 1 — Income = Total Revenue = Price

COGS 2 — Cost Of Goods Sold
Labor
Materials
Subcontractors
Equipment

EXPENSES 3 — General Expenses
Office Expenses
Job/Shop Expenses

NET PROFIT 4 —
INCOME
- COGS
- Expenses
NET PROFIT

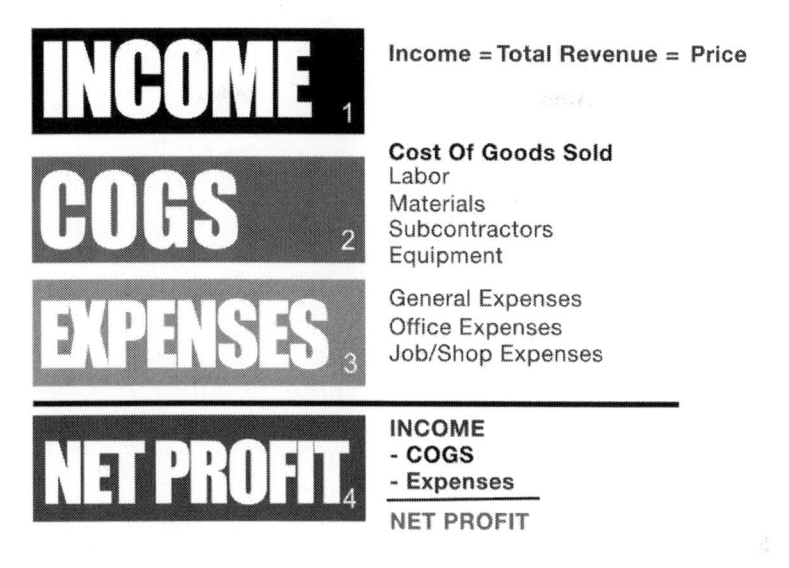

Figure 2. Sample Profit and Loss Statement for a Construction Business

The P&L is the budget for your construction business and shows the income or total revenue you have received or will receive and the COGS and expenses you have spent or will spend over a period of time.

If you think about it, the proposals you present to your customers are mini P&L statements for their projects.

In order to prepare a proposal, you estimate your COGS and apply a markup factor to those COGS that pays for the portion of expenses that the project incurs and leaves you with a net profit. The only differences between your proposals and your P&L is that you don't show your customers your COGS, expenses, and net profit; at least you shouldn't, unless you want to open up a nasty can of worms with your customers. In general, your proposals show the scope of work along with the price.

Let's go back to the first equation presented in this chapter - the most important equation:

PRICE = COSTS x MARKUP FACTOR

Construction is a cost-based business. In order to make a profit in your construction business, you must calculate your COGS and apply the appropriate markup factor so that you can pay for your expenses and have a net profit left over.

In order for the P&L to show a net profit on the bottom line, then your proposals (the mini P&Ls) have to meet the criteria above. If your individual proposals do not generate a profit, then your business never will. Your proposals can't generate a profit if you don't calculate your COGS and apply the correct markup factor.

Now I know what you're asking. "Shawn, how do I determine my markup? That is the key to making sure I have the right price, which in turn ensures I am making a profit." Hang with me here. We'll get to that. But first there's one more financial report you need to understand.

The Balance Sheet

The BALANCE SHEET shows much of the same financial information as the P&L, but there are some important differences between the two. First, the balance sheet is a statement of the financial position of a business, which states the assets, liabilities, and owner's equity at a particular point in time.

What does that mean? In a greatly simplified explanation, the balance sheet shows the net worth of the business. In contrast, the P&L shows the business' ability to generate profits.

The second difference between the balance sheet and the P&L is the way they treat time. The balance sheet summarizes the financial position of the business at a particular *point in time*. The P&L shows the revenues and expenditures during a given *period of time*.

Huh? Think of it this way: The P&L shows what you *are doing* (during a period of time). The balance sheet shows what you *have done* (up to a point in time).

The balance sheet gets its name from this equation:

Assets (stuff you own) - Liabilities (money you owe) = Owner's Equity

The two sides of the equation always balance. That's where the name comes from.

For small businesses, the balance sheet is pretty straightforward. Take the cash in your business accounts, add the estimated market value of any property you own, and subtract all debt and current obligations you have. For larger businesses, the balance sheet gets more complicated and takes a financial professional to accurately prepare.

So, let's keep it simple and focus on one area of the balance sheet - owner's equity.

Many construction business owners pay themselves through what is called an OWNER'S DRAW or owner's distribution. This distribution comes from the retained earnings of the business, which accumulates over time by generating net profits. But the owner's distribution does not show up on the P&L because it is not tied to a business expense. This distribution is accounted for on the balance sheet and is tied to the net worth of the business.

And this is a big problem for your construction business.

Here's why.

Owner distributions are your withdrawals from the business for your personal use. Owner distributions include any withdrawal that is not tied to a business expense and is paid as a distribution or dividend to a company owner. Owner's distributions are officially made from retained earnings, which is the summation of net income from prior periods, although your company actually pays you from its cash.

In other words, you don't have to work in your business to get an owner's distribution. You simply have to own the business. You can sit on a beach sipping Mai Tais and own a business.

If you do any work inside your business, like sales, design, estimating, project management, lead technician, janitor, bookkeeper, or chief bottle washer, then you should be paid a salary or a wage for the value of that work. Just like an employee would be paid.

If you work in your business and don't pay yourself the value of that work, then the money for that labor, whether it's a COGS or expense, won't show up on the P&L. If the value of that COGS (field work) or expense (office work) doesn't show up on the P&L, and the P&L is how you determine the price for your work, then you'll never be able to determine how much to charge to make a net profit.

For example:

Your P&L shows you made a $60,000 net profit after all of your COGS and expenses were deducted from your income. You worked a majority of your time as a lead carpenter in the field putting work in place and some time each week in the office running the business, but you only paid yourself with owner's distributions, and those distributions totaled $80,000. Where did the money come from?

It came from your assets, most likely, your cash on hand. How can you make a net profit of $60,000, not charge your customers for the value of the 50 to 60 hours a week you worked in your business and pay yourself $80,000?

You can't. You didn't make a net profit, at least not a positive net profit.

This is one reason why you're working like crazy, thinking you are making a profit, but you never have any cash. You're paying yourself as the owner of a business that is making a profit, but you are actually working as a non-paid employee for an unprofitable business.

This is one of the "advantages" of owning and operating a business. If you don't pay yourself, you'll still show up for work tomorrow. Try that with an employee and see what happens.

I know your accountant said that you will save some money on your taxes by paying yourself with owner's distributions, but owner's distributions are for the owners of businesses that are making profits, not for employees working in the business. Technically, this form of compensation may save you some money in taxes, but the money, the profits you are missing out on because you aren't charging enough for the value of your work is costing you a significant amount more than what you are saving in taxes.

And besides, you shouldn't have to worry about paying taxes. A profitable business will provide you with the funds to pay your taxes. You'll find out in the next few chapters just how PFC will fund all your tax liabilities.

What? You thought when I said you don't have to worry about taxes I meant you won't have to pay them. No. I just meant that you won't have to stress about finding the money in the spring or filing for that extension. Your business is going to pay for everything, including your taxes, just the way God intended.

Making the Financial Reports Work for You

Let's recap before we move on. You now understand some of the financial terms of your construction business. We defined terms like COGS and expenses, net profit and markup.

You also understand that the P&L statement (a.k.a. the income statement) shows a summary of revenues, costs, and expenditures for a given period of time and that the balance sheet shows the net worth of the company at a given point in time.

Although the P&L statement and the balance sheet show some of the same information, these two financial reports are different. You also learned that owners of a business get paid from the value of the company (shown on the balance sheet) and that employees' wages show up as a COGS or as an expense (shown on the P&L) depending on whether that employee's labor is a COGS (field work) or an expense (office/administration work).

We also learned that math is math, and math doesn't change. And we know the basic equations that determine the price of our proposals. We also know how the prices of our work add up to our total income or revenue. And we learned that these terms: price, income, and revenue are interchangeable.

The final step in making the financial reports work for your business is understanding which terms are not interchangeable.

[enter stage left: MARGIN]

In order to understand MARGIN, we need to go back to the P&L statement and look at it in greater detail.

The four categories of the P&L are:
1. INCOME
2. COGS
3. EXPENSES
4. NET PROFIT

In order to determine your price, or the income you will receive from a project, you multiply your COGS by your markup factor.

PRICE = INCOME = COGS x MARKUP FACTOR

In order to make a net profit, your markup factor must be high enough to pay for your expenses and have something left over. And this is where margin comes in.

Think about a page in a book. The space between the edge of the words and the edge of the page is called the margin.

} MARGIN

the "SPACE" between the edge of the words & the edge of the page

MARGIN

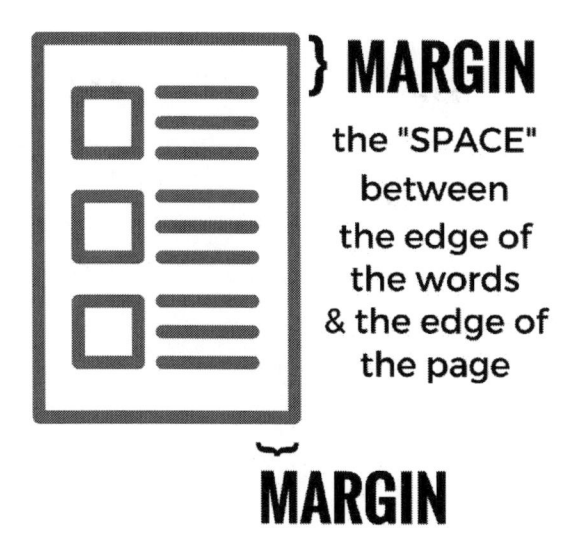

Figure 3. An Example of Margin

Your margin (gross profit) is the space between your price(income) and your COGS. This space needs to be larger than your expenses. If it is, then you will show a net profit.

NET PROFIT = (GROSS PROFIT) - EXPENSES

Or

NET PROFIT = (INCOME – COGS) - EXPENSES

The margin for your construction business is often expressed as a percentage. But in order to understand how your margin works, you first must understand what the percentages of your P&L statement mean.

Understanding the Percentages of the P&L

Any time you see a percentage, what you are really looking at is a ratio of one thing in relation to something else. This ratio can be shown as a fraction or a percentage. The fraction ¼ is the same thing as 25%.

In order to use your P&L statement to track or predict the operations of your business, you want to translate the dollar amounts of the four main categories (income, COGS, expenses, and net profit) into percentages, or ratios of the total income.

Let's use the sample P&L statement from Figure 2. Assume this is your construction business' P&L and add some dollar amounts to the categories.

INCOME $1,000,000   100%

COGS $700,000   70%

EXPENSES $250,000   25%

NET PROFIT $50,000   5%

Figure 4. Sample P&L

The income for your business is $1,000,000. Now, let's translate your income to the PERCENTAGE of TOTAL REVENUE (PTR) for your business.

I promise I'm not trying to be cute here. I am merely breaking this down, so we don't miss a step.

The total income in dollars for your business is $1,000,000. Therefore, the total income for your business in a percentage is 100%

$ TOTAL INCOME / $ TOTAL INCOME x 100% = 100%

The total income is 100% of the budget for your business. That's all the money you have to spend on the other three categories of your business during a period of time (let's say the calendar year).

Now, let's do the same for the COGS. You want to express your COGS as a percentage of your business' income. Divide your COGS in dollars by your business' income in dollars.

$ COGS / $ INCOME x 100% = $700,000 / $1,000,000 x 100% = 70%

This means that for every dollar of income you receive, you spend $0.70 on your COGS.

Next, you will apply the same method to your expenses, and express them as a percentage of your income.

$ EXPENSES / $ INCOME x 100% =

$250,000 / $1,000,000 x 100% = 25%

This means that for every dollar of income you receive, you spend $0.25 on your expenses.

And finally, you will do the same calculation for your net profit.

You know that your NET PROFIT is:

NET PROFIT = INCOME - COGS - EXPENSES

Therefore, in this example, the net profit must be 5%.

NET PROFIT = INCOME - COGS - EXPENSES

Or

NET PROFIT = 100% - 70% - 25% = 5%

Or in dollars

NET PROFIT = $1,000,000 - $700,000 - $250,000 = $50,000

A net profit of $50,000 for a business with an income of $1,000,000 is 5%.

$ NET PROFIT / $ INCOME x 100% = $50,000 / $1,000,000 x 100% = 5%

This means that for every dollar of income you receive, you generate $0.05 of net profit for the business.

The way to think about your P&L is to think in terms of percentages. If you spend more than 100% of your income on your COGS and your expenses, then you will have a negative net profit.

If you spend less than 100% of your income on COGS and expenses, then you will have a positive net profit

We will cover just how much net profit you need for your construction business in Chapter 7.

In the next chapter, we are going to solve the mystery of margin and markup and then apply what we learn to the PFC system we are going to establish for the business. But for now, let's take a deep breath. That's right. In through the nose. Out through the mouth. Let's camp out on the P&L and the balance sheet and make sure we have these things in order before moving on.

It's time to take action again. This is the doing part. Don't skip it and move on. Without a proper P&L statement, you will have to guess at the numbers. You can't guess your way to profitability. You must calculate it.

The action steps in this chapter are designed to help you understand your P&L statement. If you don't have a P&L statement, then you are going to have to make one. You need this information in order to do PFC. Don't worry if you don't have all the information. You can make some assumptions.

"Wait, Shawn. You just said that I wasn't supposed to guess. You can't guess your way to profitability."

I know. I know. But here's the difference. If you don't have certain information, then you can make an assumption and move on.

When you get better information and you know where your assumptions are, then you can go back and update the assumptions with better information. Making assumptions in the absence of information is the only way to keep moving forward.

Guessing means that we can't trace our steps back, but making an assumption can be calculated.

In the action steps on the next page, mark your assumptions (if you have any) so that when you get better information, you can go back and update your assumptions and recalculate your numbers.

Action Steps

1. Get your P&L statement for a 12-month period.*

    Hopefully you can get this from your accounting software, bookkeeper, or CPA. You will need this by the time we get to Chapter 5. If you aren't using accounting software like QuickBooks, then you need to make a P&L statement from your bank statements. Use the sample P&L statement from www.profitfirstcontractor.com as a guide.

2. Reorganize your P&L (if needed) so that all your COGS and expenses are properly accounted for in those categories. Make sure to account for any money you paid yourself in owner's distributions in your COGS and/or expenses. Note any assumptions you have so you can come back and update those assumptions later.

3. Translate the four major areas of your P&L (income, COGS, expenses, and net profit) into percentages of the total income. The income is always 100% of your P&L for that period of time. The other areas are calculated as follows:

    $ of COGS / $ of TOTAL INCOME x 100%

    $ of EXPENSES / $ of TOTAL INCOME x 100%

    $ of NET PROFIT / $ of TOTAL INCOME x 100%

* If producing your P&L statement was like pulling teeth, then you have identified the first problem you need to address. If your bookkeeper or CPA can't quickly produce this report for you, then you either have the wrong person working for you or you haven't given this person the information she needs to produce this report in a timely manner. Don't worry. We can fix that. Take a deep breath. Let's keep going.

Chapter 3

THE BIGGEST PROBLEM FOR CONTRACTORS - THE DIFFERENCE BETWEEN MARKUP AND MARGIN

I grew up in East Tennessee, but I wasn't born there. My family moved from Seattle to the South when I was three years old. Both of my parents were from the West Coast, and when we moved to Tennessee my parents went through somewhat of a culture shock. My parents have lots of funny stories about adjusting to living in the South.

For example, when our neighbors invited our family over for Sunday dinner they expected us to show up around noon. When we were a no-show, Jim (our neighbor) called and asked my dad, "Y'all gonna make it to dinner?"

After a few awkward seconds of confusion, my dad replied, "Yes. We're planning on it. What time? About 5:30?"

To which Jim replied, "Well, that's supper time. I guess we could do that, too."

In many parts of the South, especially in East Tennessee, dinner means lunch and supper means dinner. My parents thought dinner and supper both referred to the evening meal. These words seemed similar, but in actuality, these words did not mean the same thing.

Although "dinner means lunch" might be a southern *thang*, using words interchangeably that aren't interchangeable can cause confusion between the parties involved. When it comes to determining the financial health of your construction business, you must calculate, track, and project your MARKUP and MARGIN.

And these words do not mean the same thing. They should not be used interchangeably. It's like showing up at 5:30pm for Sunday dinner. You'll miss out on the good stuff.

Understanding the Difference between Markup and Margin

I was participating in a panel discussion at a national trade show, and I was asked, "If you could only teach one thing to the construction industry, what would it be?"

Without hesitation, I said, "The difference between markup and margin, and how to use them to make a profit."

In my work with construction business owners all over the world, this is the most common problem I encounter. But it is easy to solve because the solution is just simple math. Once you understand how the math of these two terms works, then you will free yourself from all the guesswork that you have been doing. What you are going to learn in the next few pages will change the way you look at your business and will give you the confidence to sell your work at the right price.

Markup is the amount of money you add to your COGS to determine your price.

Margin is the space between your price (income) and your COGS.

On your P&L you will see a line below your total COGS called GROSS PROFIT.

GROSS PROFIT = INCOME − COGS

The gross profit is all the money you have left to pay for your expenses and have a net profit left over.

"That sounds familiar. Where have I heard that before?"

The gross profit is your GROSS MARGIN (margin for short). Whether your gross profit is enough to pay for all your expenses and leave you with enough of a net profit to run a sustainable construction business has yet to be determined. So, let's determine what your margin needs to be and the markup that will yield that margin.

Margin and markup are not the same thing. They are not interchangeable.

Let's take a look at a simple example, and remember, this is just math. The numbers can change, but the way the math works is the same.

$100 DOLLAR EXAMPLE

You buy something that costs you $100.

You mark up the cost by 20%, and you sell your thing for a price of $120.

PRICE = COSTS x MARKUP FACTOR

$120 = $100 x 1.2

If the cost of your thing was $100, and you sold it for $120, then your gross profit is $20.

GROSS PROFIT = PRICE - COSTS

$20 = $120 - $100

Here is the mistake that most construction business owners make. They say something like, "I marked up my costs by 20%, therefore I made a 20% profit."

But this is wrong. You didn't make 20% profit. You make a 16.7% gross profit.

"What do you mean, Shawn?! Twenty dollars divided by one hundred dollars is 20%. You're crazy!"

Before you throw this book across the room or stop listening, hang with me for just a few more seconds. You're right. Twenty dollars divided by one hundred dollars is 20%, but the "$100" is your cost. You don't sell your costs. You sell your price.

Remember how we, in the previous chapter, translated your COGS into a percentage of your income (price) on the P&L statement. We divided your COGS by the income. The same thing applies here.

In order to determine the margin in this $100 example, you take your gross profit of $20 and divide by the price of $120, not the costs of $100.

Twenty dollars divided by one hundred twenty dollars is 16.7%.

MARGIN = $ GROSS PROFIT / $ PRICE x 100%

MARGIN = $20/$120 x 100% = 16.7%

If you make this mistake, dividing by the costs instead of the price, when determining the required markup for your work, then you will be losing money.

A 20% markup yields a 16.7% margin.

A 20% markup *does not* yield a 20% margin.

If you need a 20% margin to pay for your expenses and leave you with a net profit, then you will need to mark up your COGS by 25%.

COGS = $100
MARKUP FACTOR = 1.25
PRICE = $100 x 1.25 = $125
GROSS PROFIT = PRICE - COGS = $125 - $100 = $25
MARGIN = GROSS PROFIT / PRICE = $25/$125 = 20%

This is the math, and the math doesn't change. This is so important to understand and get right. Your profits and the success of your business depend on it.

The table on the next page shows you the margins that various markups produce.

MARKUP FACTOR	MARGIN %
1.15	13.04%
1.20	16.67%
1.25	20.00%
1.30	23.08%
1.35	25.93%
1.40	28.57%
1.45	31.03%
1.50	33.33%
1.67	40.12%
1.83	45.36%
2.00	50.00%
2.25	55.56%
2.50	60.00%

Figure 5. Margin and Markup Table

Memorize this table.

Go to www.ProfitFirstContractor.com for a pdf that you can download, print out, and tape it to your computer screen. Hell, you should frame it and hang it on your office wall. Use it every time you prepare a proposal. Stop leaving money on the table.

Moving Forward with PFC

We have covered a lot of information in the last two chapters. Let's review it one last time before we move on to implementing PFC.

1. We have reviewed the P&L statement and broken down how to categorize the four main areas of the P&L - income, COGS, expenses and net profit.
2. We have reviewed the balance sheet and defined what it is - a snapshot of your business' net worth at a given point in time.

3. We showed how an owner's distribution works, and why these distributions show up on the balance sheet and not the P&L and how this can skew the value of the net profits if not applied correctly.
4. We have calculated each of the four main categories of the P&L statement in terms of the total income expressed as percentages.
5. Based on the percentages of each of the four main categories, you can now determine the markup factor you need to apply to your COGS to get your income (price).

    MARKUP FACTOR = INCOME / COGS

    Or

    INCOME (PRICE) = COGS x MARKUP FACTOR

6. We have defined what markup and margin are, the differences between the two, and how to use them to determine your price (income).

Now you are ready to start implementing PFC by taking the initial assessment.

Actually, there's one last thing we need to do before we perform the initial assessment.

"But you said I was ready, Shawn!"

Trust me, we're getting there. We just need to make sure we define a couple of terms that will be used throughout the remainder of this book.

PFC Terms and Definitions - Do not skip this!

The Profit First formula is:

Sales - Profits = Expenses

The result of applying this formula to any business is that it forces you to prioritize your profits first and operate a business on what's left. If a business can't operate on the leftovers (the expenses), then the business must raise its prices (sales), cut expenses, or a combination of the two. But you don't mess with the profits. Profit is the priority.

In general, this formula works for any business. But you aren't running just any business. You are running a construction business, and we have just spent the last several pages defining terms for a construction business. So, let's define some specific terms for PFC that will establish consistency for the remainder of this book.

The term "expenses" in the Profit First formula means all of a business' expenditures - all the money that gets spent. The term "expenses" for a construction business means anything that is not a COGS. So, let's replace the term "expenses" in the Profit First formula with the PFC term "EXPENDITURES." Therefore "expenses" in the Profit First formula means "expenditures", and "expenditures" in the PFC formula is (COGS + expenses).

EXPENDITURES = (COGS + EXPENSES)

Also, the term "sales" in Profit First means income. So, let's use income in the PFC formula. Finally, "profits" in the Profit First formula means net profits. We are going to use net profit in the PFC formula. With the terms translated from the general Profit First language to the PFC language, the PFC formula can be written as:

INCOME - NET PROFITS = EXPENDITURES

"Shawn, you're being kind of picky here, aren't you?"

Yes, but absolute clarity matters. We need to make sure we are using the correct terms because in the next chapter we are going to start developing your plan to finally make profits for your construction business, and these specific terms will be used.

That was a lot of information, but thanks for sticking it out. This is the hardest part. Congratulations, you made it. Understanding how to read the financial reports of your construction business is something many construction business owners never learn, and many construction business owners can't explain the difference between margin and markup.

Now you can. You are light years ahead of other construction businesses.

Action Steps

1. Calculate your markup factor. Take the P&L you developed in the last chapter. Divide the dollar amount of total income (the top line revenue, the price for all the work) by the dollar amount of your COGS. This will give you the markup factor for that given period of time.

2. Analyze your net profit. In the last chapter you included any owner's draws you took as either a COGS or expense or a combination of both. Now look at your net profit. If your net profit is negative, then you need to increase your markup factor to make that number positive.

3. Recalculate your markup factor. If your net profit is negative, increase your markup factor and multiply your new markup factor times your COGS to get a new income.

4. Keep repeating step 3 until the income is high enough to pay for your COGS and expenses and leave you with a positive net profit.

    NET PROFIT = INCOME - COGS - EXPENSES

5. This is the price (income) you needed to charge in order to make a net profit given your business' COGS and expenses. This may be a shock, but this is the math.

Chapter 4

HOW PROFIT FIRST FOR CONTRACTORS WORKS - SETTING UP YOUR ACCOUNTS

In June of 2016, my wife declared to me that we were going to have a lifestyle change. I am fairly certain that my heart stopped beating for a solid three seconds. The last time she said something like this was two years earlier, and she informed me that she was pregnant…again. We already had four boys, and we had decided that we were done having kids. God has an interesting sense of humor. Although we had mentally decided that we were not going to have more kids, we didn't do anything physical to prevent it from happening. In fact, we kept doing the same thing that led to the creation of the boys. I don't think I need to go any further with this story. I will let you fill in the details. But in the spring of 2015, our little baby girl was born on my 41st birthday, a girl amongst four boys and on my birthday. I told you God has a sense of humor.

And there I was again, one year later - a deer in the headlights. Time stopped. My heart stopped. My mind was racing. I knew that we had made it almost impossible to have another child. I was there. My wife was there. A urologist and his nurse were there. I remember the Valium. I remember the hospital gown. I remember the ice pack. I remember when the doctor called and gave me the all-clear, verbal "you're sterile" high-five.

The lifestyle change my wife had declared was not another child, but a change in what we ate and the manner in which we ate it. I hate diets because they never work. You get some initial progress but then life happens, and you resort back to old habits. My wife informed me that we weren't doing a diet. Not only were we going to change what we ate, but we were also going to change how we prepared what we ate. My relationship with food was about to change.

We started the Whole30 program. This program is not a diet, but, according to the website, "a short-term nutrition reset, designed to help you put an end to unhealthy cravings and habits, restore a healthy metabolism, heal your digestive tract, and balance your immune system."

Basically, you strip down your diet to a few core categories of food and eat nothing else for thirty days. Then you can slowly add back in items and you'll be able to tell which items have an adverse effect on the way you feel.

Here's a very general list of what we could consume:
- Meat
- Vegetables
- Fruit
- Seafood
- Eggs (thank God for eggs!!!)
- Water, tea, coffee.

That's unsweetened tea and black coffee. Yuck.

There's a lot of stuff you can't eat, but that list is way too long. But here's the basic list: no sugar, no grains, no legumes, and no dairy. I know it sounds horrible, but it wasn't as bad as it looks.

The great part of Whole30 is that it breaks down what you can eat into the basics. It makes you look at your nutrition in a new light. When you get very clear on what you can eat - meats, veggies, fruit and fish - then you don't have to worry about counting calories or cutting back. You can do this. You can't do that.

Profit First for Contractors applies the same lifestyle change to your construction business. It's a way to get focused on the nutrition of your business and cut out all the stuff that doesn't matter or leaves you feeling bloated, lethargic, and unhealthy.

Let's focus on the fundamentals of running a profitable construction business.

You may have started your construction business because you wanted to be in total control of your future, find financial freedom, share a passion for your craft, or, if you're like many entrepreneurs, you just couldn't help yourself. Being your own boss is just how you were made. Whatever your *why* was for starting your construction business, the *how* you stay in business is profit.

When you make a profit in your business, then you will have to pay taxes on that profit. Like death, taxes are a fact of life. Therefore, paying your taxes is part of running a profitable construction business.

As I mentioned earlier, one of the advantages of owning a business is that you don't have to pay yourself and you'll still show up for work tomorrow.

"Advantage?! How is that an advantage, Shawn?"

Try not paying one of your employees and see if he still shows up for work. He probably won't. But you've probably worked for free quite a bit. And that's one of the reasons why you aren't as profitable as you should be. You're giving away your work for free. You need to be charging for the work you do within the company. No one starts a business so they can work for free. Therefore, paying yourself a salary for running the business, or owner's compensation (OWNER'S COMP for short), is part of operating a profitable construction business.

Finally, if you are in business then it means that you produce a product or service that you sell to customers. In order to produce that product or service you are going to have some operating expenditures (see the last chapter as to why PFC uses the word expenditures as opposed to the word expenses in *Profit First*). For a construction business the operating expenditures (OPEX for short) are your COGS and your expenses.

So that you have an idea of the basic nutrition for your construction business and understand how it works, Profit First and PFC take the nutrition analogy just a little bit further. They use a "small plates" analogy for handling your company's bank accounts. You'll establish five different checking accounts and allocate money into them to be used for specific purposes.

These are the checking accounts you will set up for your business:

1. INCOME
2. PROFIT
3. OWNER'S COMP
4. TAX
5. OPEX

You'll learn all about how each of the accounts works and how you'll manage the allocation of funds into them, but for now, let's figure out *why* these accounts are so important.

Mike explains in *Profit First* the dietary science of why this cash management system works.

Profit First Basics

> The Four Core Principles of Profit First
>
> Let's take a moment to talk dietary science. No groans, please. This stuff is fascinating.
>
> In 2012, a report by Koert Van Ittersum and Brian Wansink in the Journal of Consumer Research concluded that the average plate size in America had grown 23 percent between the years 1900 and 2012, from 9.6 inches to 11.8 inches. Running the math, the article explains that should this increase in plate size encourage an individual to consume just fifty more calories per day, that person would put on an extra five pounds of weight each year. Year after year, that adds up to a very chunky monkey.
>
> But using smaller plates is just one factor. A Twinkie on a small plate is still a Twinkie. There is more to a healthy diet, and it is based on four core principles of weight loss and nutrition.
>
> 1. Use Small Plates—Using smaller plates starts a chain reaction. When you use a small plate, you get smaller portions, which means you take in fewer calories. When you take in fewer calories than you normally would, you start to lose weight.
>
> 2. Serve Sequentially—If you eat the vegetables, rich in

nutrients and vitamins, first, they will start satisfying your hunger. When you move on to the next course—your mac and cheese or mashed potatoes (they don't count as veggies!)—you will automatically eat less. By changing the sequence of your meals by eating your vegetables first, you automatically bring a nutritional balance to your diet.

3. Remove Temptation—Remove any temptation from where you eat. People are driven by convenience. If you're anything like me, when there's a bag of Doritos sitting in the kitchen, it calls out to you constantly—even when you aren't hungry. If you don't have any junk food in the house, you're probably not going to run out to the store to get it. (That would mean putting on pants.) You're going to eat the healthy food you stocked instead.

4. Enforce a Rhythm—If you wait until you are hungry to eat, it is already too late, and you will binge. Then you are likely to eat too much and stuff yourself. You go from starving to stuffed, and back to starving again. These peaks and valleys in your hunger result in way too much calorie consumption. Instead, eat regularly (many researchers suggest five small meals a day) so that you never get hungry. Without the peaks and valleys, you will actually eat fewer calories.

These principles are effective because there's some serious psychology behind them. They work because it's how humans are wired.

Psychology of Profit First

Parkinson's Law – Filling Time with Work (Use Small Plates)

In 1955, a modern philosopher named C. Northcote Parkinson came up with the counterintuitive Parkinson's Law: that the demand for something expands to match its supply. In economics, this is called induced demand...

The more we have of something, the more of it we consume. This is true for anything from food to time.

Pop quiz!

How long does it take to do a 6-hour task?

Answer: 8 hours.

"Because with only two hours in the workday left, I don't want to start a new task. I will start on it tomorrow. Let's see what else I can work on to finish out the day." If your employees don't know that they have 6 hours to do a task, then they tend to expand the work to fill the time you allow. They aren't necessarily being unethical, just human. This is Parkinson's Law.

> The Primacy Effect: Why the First Part of Profit First Matters (Serve Sequentially)
>
> The second behavioral principle you need to understand about yourself is called the Primacy Effect. The principle is this: we place additional significance on whatever we encounter first.
>
> When we follow the conventional formula of Sales − Expenses = Profit, we are primed to focus on those first two words, Sales and Expenses, and treat profit as an afterthought. We then behave accordingly.

We push for more sales, then use the money we collect to pay expenditures. We stay stuck in the craftsman cycle, and as Mike states, "[Our focus remains on] selling to pay bills, over and over again, wondering why we never see any profit...When profit comes first, it is the focus, and it is never forgotten."

Out of Sight, Out of Mind, and Safely Put Away

When you eliminate all the processed food, food with additional sugar, and all the yummy gluten-filled food from the house, and you're left with carrots, pistachios and black coffee, then that's what you eat. You eat good food because that's all that's left.

Cash works the same way. As you walk through PFC, you are going to guarantee you make a profit by putting it in your profit account first, and then you are not going to touch it. If you don't see it, then you won't spend it. And then when it is time (we will cover how and when to disburse the profits in Chapter 8) it will be there. It will feel like a bonus.

Enforce a Rhythm and Create a Good Habits

> When you get into a rhythm with your cash management you'll have your finger on the pulse of your business. You will monitor your cash position every day by just looking at your bank account. Log in. Spend two seconds looking at your balances. Log out. You will know where you stand that quickly.
>
> [This] isn't anything new (not even to you). It is something I suspect you have been aware of—in full or at least in part—but have never done. It is the concept of "pay yourself first" meets "small plate servings" meets "Grandma's envelope-money management system" meets your preexisting natural, human tendencies.

The word rhythm is defined as: a strong, regular, repeated pattern of movement or sound. Getting into a rhythm sounds like fun. But developing good habits can be difficult. Charles Duhigg describes in his book, *The Power of Habits,* how researchers at MIT discovered a simple neurological loop at the core of every habit, a loop that consists of three parts: A cue, a routine and a reward. PFC uses the rhythm of this habit loop and creates a simple system to monitor your cash flow and make proactive decisions.

The cue: income is deposited into your income account.
The routine: the 10/25 rule (explained in Chapter 8)
The reward: cash flow management

Checking your bank balance will establish a habit of operating your construction business effectively.

Here's how you apply the four principles in *Profit First*:

Profit First Basics

1. Use Small Plates—When money comes into your main INCOME account, it simply acts as a serving tray for the other accounts. You then periodically disperse all the money from the INCOME account into different accounts in predetermined percentages. Each of these accounts has a different objective: one is for profit, one for owner compensation, another for taxes, and another for operating [expenditures]. Collectively, these are the five foundational accounts (Income, Profit, Owner's Comp, Tax, and Operating [Expenditures]), and where you should get started, but advanced users will use additional accounts, outlined in Chapter 10 [of Profit First].

2. Serve Sequentially—Always, *always* allocate money based upon the percentages to the accounts first. Never, ever, ever pay bills first. The money moves from the INCOME account to your PROFIT account, OWNER'S COMP, TAX, and OPEX (OPERATING [EXPENDITURES]). Then you pay bills only with what is available in the OPEX account. No exceptions. And if there isn't enough money left for expenses? This does *not* mean you need to pull from the other accounts. What it *does* mean is that your business is telling you that you can't afford those [expenditures] and need to get rid of them. Eliminating unnecessary [expenditures] will bring more health to your business than you can ever imagine.

3. Remove Temptation—Move your PROFIT account and other "tempting" accounts out of arm's reach. Make it really hard and painful to get to that money, thereby removing the temptation to "borrow" (i.e., steal) from yourself. Use an accountability mechanism to prevent access, except for the right reason.

> 4. **Enforce a Rhythm**—Do your allocations and payables twice a month (specifically, on the tenth and twenty-fifth). Don't pay only when there is money piled up in the account. Get into a rhythm of allocating your income and paying bills twice a month so that you can see how cash accumulates and where the money really goes. This is controlled recurring and frequent cash flow management, not by-the-seat-of-your-pants cash management.

Changing Your Relationship with Your Cash

When I read *Profit First*, poolside in that Wyoming hotel, I knew that this was the system that my clients and every construction business owner needed to make their businesses profitable. *Profit First* gave me a framework and system for helping construction business owners organize and operate their businesses in a healthy way. But *Profit First* needed to be translated into a specific format for the construction industry. That's why I am writing this book. To take the general principles that Mike designed in *Profit First* and make them specific and executable for construction business owners.

After my wife and I completed Whole30 in the summer of 2016, not only did our bodies change – my wife lost ten pounds and I shed twenty – but our relationship with food also changed. Food was no longer something we craved. Food – healthy, clean, and organic food – became fuel for our bodies.

By eliminating everything from our diet except the basics of meat, veggies, fruit, seafood, eggs, and water, I became aware that my body didn't like dairy. My brain loves ice cream, but my body does not. Now that I am aware of that, it doesn't mean that I don't miss my favorite dessert of warm brownies and vanilla ice cream. I do. But I like not being curled up in the fetal position from stomach cramps more than the flavor of that wonderful dessert combination.

As contractors, we all like tools. We are tool junkies. PFC helps show you that although having the latest tool is nice (the emotional equivalent of the brownies and ice cream), making a profit, paying yourself, and managing your cash flow is better than the temporary high of that tool purchase.

When I refined Mike's Profit First system and started teaching the PFC system to my clients, they saw immediate changes in their businesses.

Remember Janice and Kelly Stitzer? They saw a 60% increase in profitability within a year. Charles Humber is a general contractor in Sarasota, Florida. Charlie started saying "no" to the wrong clients and "yes" to the right ones because he saw how this simple change affected his numbers. PFC gave him his time back and because he took his profits first, he now has more money and is paying himself exactly what he needs to thrive.

In the coming pages, I will share success stories about people who broke out of the craftsman cycle and turn a profit every month. You'll meet business owners like Ken Alger, who owns K. Alger Woodworking in Rhode Island. Here's what Ken told me about his experience implementing PFC in his business:

> Profit First changed the way that I looked at business and how my business is run today. The struggle prior to Profit First was one of constant stress and headaches wondering if there was enough money to go around. Once I implemented Profit First in my business, the stress was lifted after the first month. The system allows you to figure out the exact percentages to allocate to run a profitable business. Just knowing that every part of a deposit check was to be allocated to specific bank accounts to cover all operating [expenditures] was enough to put my mind at ease.
>
> Profit First changes your mindset. It helps you realize that both you and your business need to make money to sustain a better lifestyle. Implementing Profit First helps you attain your goals in a sustainable way and provides a system for operating your business day-to-day. With the day-to-day taken care of, I can focus on the future of my business.
>
> Before Profit First I was always in panic mode when tax time came. After implementing PFC, I have money in our taxes account each quarter and the ability to deal with

other surprises that might come up. Paying my taxes is no longer a burden.

Ken has been able to remove the burden of owning a construction business and free himself from the worry of not knowing where the money is going. This may seem like a huge goal, but when you break your business down the PFC way, then you'll realize that the key to success is setting small goals.

Setting Small Goals

One of the first questions I get about PFC is, "How can I set aside my profit if I've never made any?" This answer is simple: Start small.

I once heard on a podcast that the way to establish a good habit is to set a small goal. A goal so small it's impossible to fail. The example they discussed on the podcast was flossing your teeth. If you want to start flossing your teeth, commit to flossing one tooth. I know it sounds ridiculous, but that's the point. If you are going to establish the habit, then just start with one tooth. Anyone can do that. If that's the goal, then it's almost impossible to fail. But achieving that one small goal will lead to the habit of putting yourself in that place (in front of the mirror) with the tools (floss) you need to accomplish the bigger goal - healthy gums and teeth.

Here's Mike's example from Profit First on setting small goals:

> If you get a $1,000 deposit, I am telling you, starting today, to transfer $10 into your PROFIT account. If you could run your business off $1,000, you can surely run it off $990.

> If you get $20,000 in deposits, you transfer $200 into you PROFIT account. If you can run your business off $20,000 you absolutely can run it off $19,800. You'll never miss that one percent. That's just one percent.

I agree. That's flossing one tooth.

When you take that small action, Mike says:

> [S]omething magical will happen. You will start proving the system to yourself. You won't get rich overnight this way, but you will get a wealth of confidence. You will have a flavor of how powerful it is to reserve your profit in advance. Your job is to stick with this small step for a while. Watch your profit accumulate. Yes, it is notably small, but it is profit nonetheless. The goal here is to win over your mind. The goal is for you to realize that this unfamiliar process of taking your profit first isn't so scary after all.

Once you overcome that fear, then you are free to grow. You aren't held back any longer.

Action Steps*

1. "Open a new account: PROFIT. For simplicity's sake, make it a checking account. Don't worry about the insignificant interest implications of savings and other accounts. Your goal for now is to get started immediately and decisively." (*Yes, I told you to do this in Chapter 1, but you forgot didn't you? Do it now.*)

2. "Transfer 1 percent of your current money into the PROFIT account. You have 'seeded' the account. Don't touch it. Never transfer it. Just let it sit for now."

3. Set up four additional accounts: Income, Tax, Owner's Comp, and **OPEX.

4. Put any new deposits into the Income account.

*   Steps 1 and 2 come directly from *Profit First*

**   Since you already have an existing checking account set up for your business from which you pay your bills, you may want to rename this account the OPEX account.

Chapter 5

BECOMING A PROFIT FIRST CONTRACTOR - INITIAL ASSESSMENT

In the last chapter you met Ken Alger, owner of K. Alger Woodworking. He is one of the most self-determined business owners I have ever had the pleasure of working with, and Ken runs his businesses with military-type precision and discipline. He would say his discipline comes from the fact that "the numbers don't lie." But I think it comes from his former career as a professional hockey player. That's right. Ken played hockey at an elite level. You don't become a professional hockey player by chance. You get invited to play at that level because you put in the hard work, time on the ice, and you get the crap kicked out of you for years.

All the time, effort, and discipline it takes to become a professional hockey player doesn't guarantee success once you reach that level. All that time, effort and discipline lays the foundation for an opportunity to play at an elite level. It just gets you an invitation to the dance. Once you're there, you have to step up your game if you want to survive.

Likewise, setting up the PFC bank accounts lays the foundation for your success, but that's not enough. You have to put in the hard work. You've arrived at the dance. Now it's time to perform.

Prepping the Foundation

By this point in the book, you should have your five foundational accounts set up at your bank. If you haven't actually taken that step, stop right here, right now, and do it.

"But Shawn, I am loving PFC, and I want to know what comes next. I can't put the book down. I'll set the accounts up later. I want to keep reading."

I understand that you want to keep going, but here's the risk you run. As we get into the details of PFC, you are going to want to come up with shortcuts you think will make life easier or you'll say, "that doesn't really apply to my situation." You can certainly customize the PFC system to fit the exact needs of your construction business in any season or situation, but that will come later. First you must start with a good foundation.

Get your bank accounts set up - income, profit, tax, owner's comp, and OPEX. For simplicity, set these up as checking accounts at your bank.

You can read on, but only if you promise you will set up these accounts within the next 24 hours.

I also recommend that you read Chapter 3 in *Profit First* (if you haven't already) to learn more about setting up your bank accounts. Mike gives you step-by-step instructions on what to do and which accounts to use and how to avoid fees at your bank. If you haven't read Mike's *Profit First*, you should. It goes in to some deep detail about how to implement an advanced Profit First System for your business. But until then you can download the first five chapters of Mike's book, Profit First, at www.ProfitFirstContractor.com. Review the information specifically about the bank accounts.

Streamlining Your Cash

In my first book, *The Paperwork Punch List*, I show you how to implement some systems to get your construction business operating more effectively and efficiently. One of the first things I discuss in that book is increasing your sales by pre-qualifying your prospects and eliminating free estimates.

Without sales, there is no business. There are no profits. That's where your construction business starts. The same thing applies to PFC. The income your business generated last year, or over the last couple of years, is where we are going to start.

Now I know that one of the reasons your business suffers is because you have never been able to understand and use the financial reports produced by your accountant or accounting system. But we have already started to change that. We reviewed what your P&L statement and balance sheet are and what they tell you about your business. We are going to put that knowledge to use in this chapter and create an initial assessment for your construction business. This may seem difficult if you don't have accurate information, but don't worry about that either. We can make some assumptions, fill in the blanks, and at least get a rough working sense of where your business is.

When I am working with clients and coaching them through the numbers of their construction businesses, there's usually some information that is unknown or hasn't been tracked. When you're all alone, this uncertainty becomes a roadblock. But you're not alone anymore. You have me, and in Chapter 11, I am going to give you the resources and support you need to successfully implement PFC. But for now, it's okay to make some assumptions.

The key to the initial assessment is just doing it. Don't be fearful of the unknowns. Make your assumptions and keep going. As long as you are aware of what those assumptions are, then you can go back and replace those assumptions with more accurate data later. The initial assessment will help identify the areas of your business where you need more information and the framework will paint the overall picture of your construction business.

Let's get started. Let's dance.

The Initial Assessment

Here's how Mike describes the initial assessment:

Profit First Basics

> [PFC] is a cash-management system, not an Accounting (capital A - think GAAP) system. We don't do anything on accrual or any of that funny-money stuff. It is really simple: Did you get the cash or not? And did you spend the cash or not? That's it. Nothing else really matters unless cash happens. So that is why our focus is exclusively on cash. If you are wondering how [this system] addresses depreciation or accounts receivable, you are still thinking funny money. We are only going to measure actual cash transactions. Money in. Money out. Real money. Period.
>
> Before you start the [Initial] Assessment, get your P&L from your last full year in business. Get the tax returns for each owner in the business for the tax period for that year. Get your balance sheet for the year-end of that year. Your accounting software (if you use one) can spit this stuff out easily; everything but your tax returns. If you don't have access to a balance sheet or your P&L, that's OK; we can still get darn close. Are you ready? You have no excuses. You must proceed with this.

This is your wake-up call, PFC style.

Figure 6 is the PFC Initial Assessment form. This form is similar to the Initial Assessment form in *Profit First* but with one major addition - PFC Translations.

Complete this form right now! Do not wait. Do not pass go. Do it now. It's important.

Remember in Chapter 2 when we walked through the four major categories of your P&L statement, and how we developed the percentages of your total revenue, COGS, expenses and net profit in terms of total revenue? We are going to do the same thing for the initial assessment and translate the Profit First numbers of "REAL REVENUE" (a Profit First term, not an accounting term), net profit, tax, owner's comp, and expenses into a percentage of total revenue (PTR). This will allow you to compare your initial assessment numbers to your P&L statement.

Doing this "translation" will ensure that we are comparing apples to apples. The P&L categories can be expressed as percentages of total revenue and we want the PTR of the initial assessment to be expressed in the same way.

	ACTUAL	TAP of REAL REVENUE	PF$ of REAL REVENUE	DELTA	FIX	PFC TRANSLATION PFC ACTUAL PTR (% of TOTAL REVENUE)	PFC RECOMMEND PTR (% of TOTAL REVENUE)
TOTAL REVENUE	B3					100%	100%
MATERIALS & SUBS	B4					G4	H4
REAL REVENUE	B5		100%				
NET PROFIT	B6	C6	D6	E6	F6	G6	H6
OWNER'S COMP	B7	C7	D7	E7	F7	G7	H7
TAX	B8	C8	D8	E8	F8	G8	H8
OPERATING EXPENDITURES	B9	C9	D9	E9	F9	G9	H9
TOTAL OPEX						C10	H10

Figure 6. Profit First for Contractors Initial Assessment Form

You can build this simple spreadsheet to calculate the PFC initial assessment or write directly in this book. Also, you can go to www.ProfitFirstContractor.com and download a printable copy and an .xls file if you want. I have listed the actual cell numbers on this form for your reference if you would like to build this form in a spreadsheet.

In *Profit First*, Mike uses the term "real revenue" to describe the real dollars that any business actually manages. Every business receives money as income. Some of that money goes right back out the door to subcontractors and materials. The difference between the income a business receives and dollars that go to subcontractors and materials is what Mike calls real revenue.

Real revenue is not COGS. It's more like the actual cash you manage.

$ REAL REVENUE = $ TOTAL INCOME - $ SUBS - $ MATERIALS

This is step one in the initial assessment, and this works in general for many businesses. But the terms "subcontractors" and "materials" mean something a little different for a construction company. If your business produced and sold widgets, and you used subcontractors to produce some portion of your product, then the cost of those subs and the materials that went into producing widgets (the same product or service) remains pretty constant.

But you are running a construction business. Every project, meaning every opportunity for income, can be different. The cost of the subcontractors and materials could vary greatly from project to project. On one project, 50% revenue for that project might be spent on subcontractors and materials. On another, you may spend 30% on subcontractors and materials. That's why the real revenue from *Profit First* needs to be translated into more specific terms for PFC.

With that said, let's do your initial assessment the Profit First way, then translate those numbers into the PFC system*.

The steps listed below and in the next chapter were modified from Profit First. Mike's original words and intent are contained in text boxes, and additional comments and modifications for PFC made by me are listed below the text boxes for clarity. The intent is to attribute the content to Mike and Profit First and note the differences for PFC.

Here we go:

B3

> 1. In the Actual column, cell [B3], enter your Top Line Revenue for the last twelve full months. This is your total revenue from sales, and… should be the top line (or near it) on your P&L statement. One of the common labels for the top line is Total Income, Total Sales, Revenue, Sales, or Net Sales.

B4

> 2. Put the cumulative amount of the cost of materials (not labor) [and the cost of the subcontractors] for the last full twelve months in the Material & Subs cell [B4]. This is not, I repeat, this is not the same as Cost of Goods Sold. This is only for materials [and subcontractor costs].
>
> …Subcontractors are people who work for you on a project basis, but have the ability to work autonomously and have the ability to work for others. You don't pay them on payroll; you pay them their project fee, commission, or hourly rate, and they handle their taxes, benefits, etc., themselves.

Do not input the amount of labor for your own employees in this cell.

> 3. If you are a service [provider] and the majority of your services are provided by your employees (yourself included), [and you don't sell materials,] put $0 in cell [B4].

If you are a specialty contractor ("subcontractor") and provide mostly labor to your customers, then put $0 in this cell.

> 4. If your material or subcontractor costs are less than 25 percent of your Top Line Revenue, put a $0 in cell [B4]. (We will account for these…in the operating [expenditures]).

Wait! We don't want to do that in PFC. You have done all the hard work to get these numbers together, let's make sure we use them. Even if your materials and subcontractor costs are less than 25%, then enter that dollar amount in cell B4.

> 5. If you are unsure of what to put in the Material & Subs section, put $0. Do not overthink this. And do not use it to make nominal adjustments. The goal here is only to adjust your company's revenue to represent what it really

> makes as revenue if the majority of cost is for materials, supplies, or subcontractors. Again, if you are even a wee bit unsure, put $0 in Material & Subs (cell [B4]). It will serve you better in the long run by making you more critical of your costs.

B5

> 6. Now subtract your Material & Subs number from your Top Line Revenue to calculate your Real Revenue. If you put an n/a in the Material & Subs section, just copy the Top Line Revenue number to the Real Revenue cell [B5].
>
> 7. The goal here is to get you to your Real Revenue number. This is the real money your company makes. For the other stuff—subs, materials, etc.—you may make a margin, but it isn't the core driver of profitability because you have little control over it.

This can be a rude awakening for construction business owners.

The homebuilder that has top line sales of $2,000,000 but has $800,000 in material costs and another $700,000 in subcontractor costs is really a $500,000 business.

The real revenue number is the Profit First way to understand the amount of money you are really managing.

> Real Revenue is different from gross profit, in that Real Revenue is your total revenue minus the materials and subcontractors utilized to create and deliver the service or product. Gross profit, on the other hand, is an accounting term calculated as [Income - COGS]. It is a subtle difference but a critically important one.
>
> Gross profit includes a portion of your employees' time and your time [labor]. But the important thing is this: you will generally pay your employees for their time regardless of whether you have a bad sales day or good one. You will likely pay them the same if they [perform a task] in four hours or five.

BECOMING A PROFIT FIRST CONTRACTOR 79

To simplify things, PFC categorizes any employees, full- or part-time, as a cost of the business operations (OPEX), whether that employee is performing work that is classified as a COGS or as an expense. This distinction is only for the initial assessment and to determine the real revenue. You'll see in just a few pages how we are going use the real revenue number to set some guidelines.

Focus on the cost that you incur in materials and subs when calculating your real revenue for the initial assessment. This will help keep the numbers clear.

B6

> 8. Now that we know your Real Revenue, let's start with profit first. (See how that works?) Write down your actual profit from the last twelve months in the Profit cell [B6]. This is the cumulative profit you have sitting in the bank, or have distributed to yourself (and/or partners) as a bonus on top of—but not to supplement—your salary.
>
> If you think you have a profit, but it is not in the bank and was never distributed to you as a bonus, this means you don't really have a profit. (If it turns out that you have less profit than you thought you would, it's likely you used it to pay down debt from previous years…)

Warning: If you have a net profit shown on the bottom of your P&L statement, but your salary for performing work within your construction business does not show up in either the COGS or the expenses, then you must account for what you paid yourself. If this is the case, then you most likely do not have the net profit listed at the bottom of your P&L. Deduct any amount you paid yourself for the work you did within your business from the net profit, and put that difference in cell B6.

B7

> 9. In the Owner's Comp cell [B7], put down how much you paid yourself (and any other owners of the business) these past twelve months in regular payroll distributions,

> not profit distributions.

Warning: Remember from Chapter 2, owner's distributions are not a salary. They are a share of the profits, no matter what your CPA says. In order for you to make a profit in your business, you have to start facing facts. If the way in which you compensate yourself for the work you do in your business is through owner's distributions (a.k.a. draws), then you are (in effect) stealing from the company. You'll never make a profit this way.

B8

> 10. In the Tax cell [B8], put down how much Tax your company has paid on your behalf. This is critical: This is not how much you have paid in taxes. This is how much money your company paid (or reimbursed you) in taxes. Tax is both the income tax of all the owners and any other corporate taxes. The likelihood that your company paid your taxes for you is very low (we'll fix that, too). So chances are you will put a big fat $0 in that section, too. If your income taxes were deducted from your paycheck from the company, or at the end of the year you had to scratch together cash out of your pocket, the company definitely did not pay your taxes and a big $0 goes in cell [B8].

B9

> 11. In the Operating [Expenditures] cell [B9], add up the total expenses your business paid for the last twelve months—everything except your Profit, Owner's Comp, Tax, and any materials and subcontractors that you have already accounted for.

Take a look at your P&L statement for the past twelve months. You should have listed "Total Expenses." Also you should see your "Total COGS." You can determine your OPEX for cell B9 by adding the "Total Expenses" to the "Total COGS" and subtracting the amount for materials and subcontractors (cell B4).

OPEX = TOTAL EXPENSES + COGS - MATERIALS - SUBCONTRACTORS

Now, here is where people get confused. It's okay if the numbers don't match up perfectly. This is not accounting, and you don't need to reconcile to the penny. This is simply a system that gets us in the ballpark of where we are, and then tells us where we need to start going. The goal is *not* to have perfect numbers; it is just to understand roughly where we stand now. And with that understanding we can start working on a profit plan for your business. This is simply a starting point. As we implement [PFC] over time, we will automatically adjust and nail the perfect numbers for your business. Just get started.

Check your work by adding up your Profit [B6], Owner's Comp [B7], Taxes [B8], and Operating [Expenditures B9] to see if you get your Real Revenue number [B5]. If you don't get this number, something is off. Double-check your numbers to see if you missed something. Once you make sure all the numbers are as accurate as possible, adjust the Operating [Expenditures] number up or down to get the Real Revenue to balance. This makes many accounting professionals squeamish, but again, the goal is just to get in the ballpark; we aren't looking to master accounting here. Now add your Real Revenue to the Materials & Subs costs and you should get the Top Line Revenue number. Make sure it all squares out. Now that we have the hard work done in the first column, we can plug in the easy stuff.

C6-C9

12. Next, enter the Profit First percentages in the TAP column based upon your Real Revenue Range (fill in cells [C6 through C9]). Use the percentages in Figure [7].

Mike calls these percentages TAPs (Target Allocation Percentages), "the percentage of each deposit that will be allocated to different elements of our business."

> TAPs are not your starting point; TAPs are the targets you are moving toward. For example, if your Real Revenue for the last twelve months is $722,000, you should use column C from Figure [7]. If your business has $225,000 in Real Revenue, use column A. If you run a division (or have your own company) that does $40,000,000, use column F.

But instead of using the TAPs to determine the amount of each deposit, we are going to use the TAPs to determine a dollar amount for each of these areas of your construction business, and then translate that dollar amount to a percentage of total revenue (PTR).

The PTRs are the percentages of each deposit that will be allocated to the different elements of your business.

The reason PFC uses this additional step is because the TAPs of *Profit First* don't include the amount of money spent on subcontractors and materials. We need the PFC system to work without subtracting the amount of subs and materials out of each deposit we receive and then disbursing the money based on a percentage of *real revenue*. We want to disburse the money based on a percentage of *total revenue*.

PFC is going to use the PTR for our allocations, not the TAPs. TAPs are Profit First. PTRs are the PFC version of TAPs.

For example, if you receive a $10,000 deposit check for a project, you need to know how much of that check goes to net profit, tax, owner's comp accounts, and so on without trying to figure out how much of that $10,000 is allocated to subcontractors and materials.

Once we use the TAPs to determine the PTRs, then we know that when that $10,000 check comes in we will put 8% into profit, 5% into tax, 10% into owner's comp, and 77% into total OPEX.

Just to be clear, I will say it again. The allocation percentages in PFC are percentages of the total revenue (PTR). The target allocation percentages (TAPs) in *Profit First* are percentages of the real revenue.

Translating the TAPs into PTRs simplifies the PFC system for a construction company.

	A	B	C	D	E	F
REAL REVENUE RANGE	$0-$250K	$250K-$500K	$500K-$1M	$1M-$5M	$5M-$10M	$10M-$50M
REAL REVENUE	100%	100%	100%	100%	100%	100%
NET PROFIT	10%	20%	25%	25%	25%	20%
OWNER'S COMP	45%	25%	20%	10%	10%	7%
TAX	15%	15%	15%	15%	15%	15%
OPERATING EXPENDITURES	30%	40%	40%	50%	50%	58%

Figure 7. Profit First Target Allocation Percentages (TAPs) Based on Real Revenue

I know it might seem like I am repeating myself, but I want to make sure you understand this subtle difference. Like the difference between dinner and supper, understanding the meaning of these terms is very important.

PFC uses Mike's Profit First TAPs based on real revenue to produce a dollar amount, and that dollar amount is used to develop a percentage of total revenue (PTR) for the allocations.

Enough of that. Let's make sure we have our numbers squared away before we move on.

Action Steps:

Just like in *Profit First*:

> This entire chapter is really one big action step, so if you have not yet completed [the first two columns in the] Initial Assessment…, then do it now. Can you get a lot out of this book if you table this exercise for when you have more time or feel up to facing reality? Sure. Will you get the most out of reading this book and see results quickly if you [wait until later]? Nope. So stop right now and do it. I'm waiting . . . do it now.

Chapter 6

COMPARING APPLES TO APPLES

I operate an international coaching and consulting business. It's not that impressive. Technically, I became "international" when I landed my first Canadian client. There wasn't much difference in my approach with her as compared to my American clients. The numbers were still the numbers, the math was still math, and she spoke English, (even though Canadians say "PRO-jekt" instead of "präj-ekt").

Fast forward a few months and I started coaching Mihkel Laks, a general contractor in Sweden. Now that's international. Mihkel struggled with many of the same issues that American and Canadian contractors face. He was caught in the Swedish version of the craftsman cycle – "hantverkscykeln."

Before we developed his pricing strategy, I asked him to send me his financial reports. Whoa! That was a surprise. Although Mihkel spoke excellent English, his reports were in Swedish.

"Duh, Shawn. He lives in Sweden. What did you think?"

I had no idea what the words on his P&L meant. The basic structure was familiar, but I didn't understand the words. I needed a translator.

Thank God for Google translate.

I spent about an hour copying the Swedish words from Mihkel's P&L, pasting them into Google, and translating them into English. Translating the P&L from Swedish into English simplified the analysis of the numbers.

We developed a pricing strategy that created the margins Mihkel needed for his construction business and designed the allocations for his PFC system based on a percentage of his total revenue.

'Percentage of total revenue' is 'andel av totala intäkterna' for my Swedish readers.

In this chapter, we are going to complete the initial assessment and pick back up where we left off in the last chapter. By the end of this chapter we are going to use the numbers from your P&L, develop TAPs recommended in Profit First, and translate the dollar amounts produced by the TAPs into the percentages of total revenue (PTRs) that PFC uses going forward.

Understanding this translation is key to simplifying your PFC system. And it doesn't matter if you speak English, Swedish, or Canadian, translating your numbers into a percentage of total revenue will greatly simplify how you view your business.

I have defined many terms in this book in order for you to have an understanding of how Profit First relates to your financial statements. Profit First has its own language, and some of that language sounds vaguely familiar, like other financial language you may have heard. That's why it is important to translate certain words to ensure that there is no confusion. Keep this in mind as we finish the initial assessment.

	ACTUAL	TAP of REAL REVENUE	PF$ of REAL REVENUE	DELTA	FIX	PFC TRANSLATION PFC ACTUAL PTR (% of TOTAL REVENUE)	PFC RECOMMEND PTR (% of TOTAL REVENUE)
TOTAL REVENUE	B3					100%	100%
MATERIALS & SUBS	B4					C4	H4
REAL REVENUE	B5	100%					
NET PROFIT	B6	C6	D6	E6	F6	C6	H6
OWNER'S COMP	B7	C7	D7	E7	F7	C7	H7
TAX	B8	C8	D8	E8	F8	C8	H8
OPERATING EXPENDITURES	B9	C9	D9	E9	F9	C9	H9
TOTAL OPEX						C10	H10

Figure 6. Profit First for Contractors Initial Assessment Form

D6-D9

> 13. In the PF $ column, multiply that Real Revenue number by the TAP for each row and write down the number in the corresponding PF $ cell. For example, to determine your PF $ [Net] Profit, multiply [B5] (Real Revenue) by [C6] (the [Net] Profit TAPs) to get [D6] (the *Profit First* dollar target for [Net] Profit). Do this same process to calculate each cell in the PF $.* These are your target PF dollar amounts for each category. Welcome to the moment of truth.

If this is painful, that's because we just ripped off the band-aid (more about this in Chapter 8).

*   For the following cells (D6 through D9) enter these formulas in your spreadsheet:

NET PROFIT in cell D6 enter '=B5*C6' (without the ' ')
OWNER's COMP in cell D7 enter '=B5*C7' (without the ' ')
TAX in cell D8 enter '=B5*C8' (without the ' ')
OPERATING EXPENDITURES in cell D9 enter '=B5*C9' (without the ' ')

E6-E9

> 14. In the Delta column, take your actual number and subtract the PF $ number.† This is very likely to result in a negative number for Profit or Owner's Comp or Operating [Expenditures] or all three. It is your Delta, the amount you need to make up. Negative means you are bleeding money in these sections. Sometimes it is in just one category with a problem, but in most cases businesses are bleeding out in the Profit, Owner's Comp, and Tax accounts and have a positive number (meaning excess) in Operating [Expenditures]. In other words, we are paying too little in Profit, Owner's Comp, and Taxes, and paying too much in Operating [Expenditures].

88 PROFIT FIRST FOR CONTRACTORS

†   For the DELTA cells (E6 through E9) enter these formulas in your spreadsheet:

NET PROFIT DELTA in cell E6 enter '=B6-D6' (without the ' ')
OWNER's COMP DELTA in cell E7 enter '=B7-D7' (without the ' ')
TAX DELTA in cell E8 enter '=B8-D8' (without the ' ')
OPERATING EXPENDITURES in cell E9 enter '=B9-D9' (without the ' ')

F6-F9

> 15. The Fix column (cells [F6 through F9]), will have no numbers, only the word increase or decrease next to each category. If the number in the Delta section is a negative number, put increase in the corresponding Fix cell, because we need to increase our contribution to this category to correct the Delta. Conversely, if it is a positive number in the Delta section, put decrease in the Fix cell, since this is a category where we need to spend less money in order to fix it.

Profit First for Contractors Translation Step

Now that we have determined the specific areas that we need to fix, we need to translate these fixes into numbers that are simple to use when the checks (income) roll in. In column G, we translate the Profit First TAPs into PTRs. This will tell us the allocation we need to deposit into these categories. Up to this point in the initial assessment we have used the "real revenue" to determine our TAPs. But real revenue is just a Profit First term to determine some targets. Now that we know where the targets are, let's dial in the scope, and refine our aim.

G4, G6-G9

    16. In column G, we are going to translate the actual dollar amounts in column B into a PTR. We used the dollar amount spent on materials and subcontractors to

determine our real revenue. Now we want to translate that back into a PTR. Divide cell B4 (materials and subcontractors) by B3 (total revenue) and multiply by 100%. This gives you the actual PTR for this category. Enter this percentage in cell G4. Perform this calculation for the remaining cells in column B, each time dividing the cell in column B by the total revenue in cell B3 and multiplying by 100%. Enter each of these actual PTRs in the corresponding cells in column G. (You'll notice cell G10 does not have a corresponding B cell associated with it. Don't worry about this. That's the next step.)

G10

17. We are getting closer to being able to determine our PTRs that we should allocate to our individual accounts, but we need to make one more calculation. Remember how we used the amount we spent on materials and subcontractors to determine the real revenue, and that real revenue is not the same as COGS? In order to keep the terms in this book consistent with *Profit First* and GAAP, I had to create a couple new terms. Operating expenditures was one of those terms (see Chapter 3 for the definition of that term). Here is another PFC specific term - TOTAL OPEX. Total OPEX is the operating expenditures plus materials and subcontractors.

TOTAL OPEX = OPERATING EXPENDITURES + MAT. & SUBS

I know what you may be thinking. "If I add back in my materials and subs, then this is just the addition of my COGS and expenses from my P&L."

I like that you are getting familiar with your P&L, but total OPEX is not the same. The expenses on your P&L are not the same as the operating expenditures. The expenses on your P&L include your salary (owner's comp) and might include some taxes. The PFC system pulls these numbers out of the expenses on your P&L and gives them their own bank account.

Since expenses are not the same as operating expenditures, then adding the materials and subs to the operating expenditures will not give you the same number as adding the COGS and the expenses from your P&L.

We know the PTR of our materials and subcontractors (G4) and the PTR of operating expenditures (G9). Add these two PTRs together and enter the sum into G10. This is the actual PTR that you spent on the "everything else" of your business besides net profit, tax, and owner's comp.

H4, H6-H9

18. In column H, we are going to translate the recommended dollar amounts from the Profit First TAPs into the PFC PTRs. The recommended PRT for cell H4 is the same as G4 (that PRT won't change between your actual and the recommended - it is what it is). For cells H6-H9, divide the corresponding D cell by the total revenue (B3) and multiply by 100% and enter the number in to H6 through H9 respectively.

H10

19. The final cell in the initial assessment is H10. Like the formula for cell G10, H10 is the sum of cell H4 and H9. This will give you the recommended PTR for total OPEX.

	A	B	C	D	E	F
REAL REVENUE RANGE	$0-$250K	$250K-$500K	$500K-$1M	$1M-$5M	$5M-$10M	$10M-$50M
REAL REVENUE	100%	100%	100%	100%	100%	100%
NET PROFIT	10%	20%	25%	25%	25%	20%
OWNER'S COMP	45%	25%	20%	10%	10%	7%
TAX	15%	15%	15%	15%	15%	15%
OPERATING EXPENDITURES	30%	40%	40%	50%	50%	58%

Figure 7. Profit First Target Allocation Percentages (TAPs) Based on Real Revenue

What Do These Percentages and Numbers Mean?

Mike developed the numbers in Figure 7 based his years of experience and research with countless companies all over the world. These numbers represent what Mike (and I agree with him) considers to be very healthy numbers.

Mike states:

> The percentages aren't perfect, but they are an excellent starting point. When you run your [Initial] Assessment, chances are you will find that your actual percentages are nowhere near the numbers in [Figure 7], but that is OK because these percentages are only your targets - what you will move toward. We are going to approach these targets in small steps.

The TAPs in Figure 7 are based on "real revenue" (a *Profit First* term) not total revenue (a GAAP and PFC term). In order to simplify the PFC system, we have learned how to take the Profit First TAPs based on real revenue and translate them into PFC's PTRs based on total revenues.

Let's explore what a typical construction business looks like at various total revenues.

I classify construction companies into these five categories based on total revenues. I am painting with a broad brush here. These category descriptions may not match up exactly with your construction business, but they are probably not too far off. Read the descriptions and determine which category fits your construction business.

Start Up
1. When a construction business is doing less than $250,000 in total revenue, then it is most likely in the start-up phase. There's one employee. That's you - the owner. You might have some subcontractors that you bring in from time to time, but you are doing a majority of the heavy lifting. This can be an exciting time for you since you just got started, but you're probably not making any profit. Money is coming in and money is going out. You're starting to get busy, really busy, and you can't get to all the work in a timely fashion, but you're having fun (maybe).

Wild Ride
2. At $250,000 to $500,000 in total revenue you likely have an employee, but that employee is "hired help." That person most likely can't operate independently for any

significant period of time and needs constant direction and management. You're still doing a majority of the technical work and have fully stepped into the owner/operator model. The amount of work is starting to pick up and the inefficiencies have increased. The seat-of-the-pants operation and management style start to cause schedule delays. The stresses of keeping up with the work and with your employee start to weigh on you. You feel the need for some systems but haven't had the time to implement any. Cash is tight because of the lack of systems. Fear starts to build because you think you need to hire more help, but you're concerned that you won't have enough money for another full-time position. If you are a subcontractor (providing mainly labor to a general contractor), then you probably have a small crew of employees (you plus two), and you're not sure how to split up the team into two crews because there is only one of you. You are struggling to pay yourself a regular salary because all the cash goes to paying your employees, buying materials, and keeping the jobs going. Profits are minimal because you realize that you have to increase volume in order to cover your expenses. This is a difficult place to remain. You have to get bigger (more employees, increased sales volume) or get smaller. You feel like Atlas - the entire world is on your shoulders.

Stressful
3. Between $500,000 and $1,000,000, you have some basic systems in place, but you had to increase your expenses to get there. You're able to pay yourself a regular salary but it's probably not high enough for the number of hats you wear and the hours you put in. You have multiple teams and possibly a manager of some sort (project manager, superintendent, or office manager or admin assistant). Profits are low, but consistent. You're just starting to realize the types of projects that make you money and the ones that don't. (Read Mike's book, *The Pumpkin Plan*, to understand how to get out of this rut.)

Growth
4. Once your total revenues are above $1,000,000 but less than $5,000,000, you are focused less on producing the work (you have teams for that) and more focused on building teams to support the workload. You don't spend much time on the tools anymore and focus your efforts on sales and business development. Your marketing produces predictable results and you get clarity on who your ideal clients are and what attracts these clients. You have a management team that handles the day-to-day operations of the field work and office work. You're finally able to pay yourself a market rate salary and have profits to show for it.

Legacy
5. Above $5,000,000 in total revenue, your business feels stable and established. You start thinking differently about your business and how you can scale it up and replace yourself as an employee. You start becoming just the owner and most of your compensation is from the profits generated by the business operations.

These classifications are typical and, in my experience, completely normal. Some categories are better than others. Obviously, growth and legacy companies are great because systems are in place and profits are predictable. But I don't want you to be normal. You can be profitable and thriving even in the start-up, wild ride, and stressful phases of your business. In fact, you will reach the growth and legacy phases of your business much quicker if you're profitable in the early stages of your business. PFC guarantees it.

When you set aside your profits first and learn to operate your business on what's left, you are forced to view your business operations in a sustainable way. PFC shows you how to build profit into every project. And like Mike says in Profit First, "profit is not an event. Profit is a habit." Your profit must be built into every aspect of your business.

Figure 8 is a completed example from one of my clients. This initial assessment reveals some painful things (which can be typical). This construction business has zero profit. It should be producing a net profit of near 6% based on the real revenue TAPs.

	ACTUAL	TAP of REAL REVENUE	PF$ of REAL REVENUE	DELTA	FIX	PFC ACTUAL PTR (% of TOTAL REVENUE)	PFC RECOMMEND PTR (% of TOTAL REVENUE)
TOTAL REVENUE	$1,458,830.97					100%	100%
MATERIALS & SUBS	$1,028,062.32					70.47%	70.47%
REAL REVENUE	$430,768.65	100%					
NET PROFIT	$0.00	20%	$86,153.73	-$86,153.73	INCREASE	0.00%	5.91%
OWNER'S COMP	$62,905.86	25%	$107,692.16	-$44,786.30	INCREASE	4.31%	7.38%
TAX	$0.00	15%	$64,615.30	-$64,615.30	INCREASE	0.00%	4.43%
OPERATING EXPENDITURES	$367,862.79	40%	$172,307.46	$195,555.33	DECREASE	25.22%	11.81%
TOTAL OPEX						95.69%	82.28%

Figure 8. Completed Initial Assessment for General Contractor (New Construction & Remodeling)

The owner is not paying himself enough for the size of the business and the value of the work he is doing. At $63,000, the owner would be hard pressed to find an employee with his level of experience that could run the business for that salary. This is keeping his prices artificially low. If he had to pay market value for an employee to do his job, then he would have to raise his prices. No one with that level of experience would work for that low of a salary when he could go elsewhere and get paid what he's worth.

When you make a profit, you are going to pay taxes. Even if your business does not show a profit in a given year, but you take money out of the business (either in distributions or a salary), you will pay taxes on a personal level. This is a given. This company did not set anything aside for taxes. The owner will still have to pay taxes when the taxman comes calling, and the money for taxes has to come from somewhere. Remember Peter and Paul from Chapter 1? This company is going to have to take the money from the cash flow to pay taxes when it's time. This is going to put a huge strain on the operations of the business.

The total OPEX is astronomically high. This construction company spends $0.95 of every dollar of income on its total OPEX. Ninety-five cents of every dollar of income is spent operating the business without saving for taxes or profit. This company is caught in the craftsman cycle. Every project this company performs is putting it further and further out of business.

But this doesn't have to be your construction business.

This initial assessment shows that immediate action must be taken to pull this company out of the death spiral it is in. The owner needs to start making a profit, saving for taxes, increasing his salary, and reducing total OPEX.

Profit First Basics

> The [Initial] Assessment brings clarity fast, and it can be a rude awakening. No more putting things off. No more hoping that big client, big check, or big anything will save you from the day-to-day panic. We know exactly what we need to do.

"But where is the money going to come from?" you ask. I'll show you in the coming chapters.

Action Steps:

Like the last chapter, this chapter is one big action step. Complete columns D through H in the initial assessment.

After completing the initial assessment, you may feel confused much like the first time I looked at Mihkel's Swedish financial reports. Don't worry. You're learning a new language for your business. Don't get overwhelmed.

I think Mike can encourage you from *Profit First* with these words:

> If you are feeling overwhelmed, bad about yourself and the choices you've made, or angry about the numbers you came up with in your [Initial] Assessment, there is something I want you to know: You are normal. Totally, completely, 100 percent normal...Soon enough, the feeling of being overwhelmed, the anger and frustration, will fade as your new profit habit builds.

Chapter 7

FORGET INDUSTRY STANDARDS

Do me a favor. Hold out your right hand. I'm being serious. Hold out your right hand. Now, give me a thumbs up. I promise there's a point to this. Now look at your thumb, specifically the end of your thumb. If you had to guess, what would you say is the distance between the tip of your thumb and the first joint?

Did you guess, "about an inch?"

If so, then you would be correct. You didn't need a ruler. You just kind of knew. It seemed about right. That's where the phrase "rule of thumb" comes from. The earliest appearance of this phrase in print came from a sermon where the preacher compared parishioners to builders, "who build by guess and rule of thumb, and not by square and rule."[3]

The initial assessment you performed in the previous chapters is a rule of thumb you can apply to your construction business. Applying rules of thumb to your business is an efficient way to simplify the calculations or analyses as long as these rules are based on actual data.

The initial assessment is designed to help you identify the areas of your construction business that need improvement. Many construction business owners start off the initial assessment with a big fat $0 in the net profit and tax cells. (Don't beat yourself up. This is completely normal. You are not alone.)

Now that you are aware of the holes in your business, you may feel the need to jump head first into PFC and start dumping money into these accounts to try to make up for lost time. Don't make that mistake. If you have never made a profit in your

---

[3] O'Conner, P. and Kellerman, S. (2010). Origins of the specious. New York: Random House Trade Paperbacks.

business, then it will be difficult to make the leap to the PTRs that the Initial Assessment recommends.

Instead of trying to make the huge leap to sustainable profits this instant, let's identify a few common mistakes that can hamper your implementation of the PFC system.

Three Common Problems

1. **Following industry standards.** Your construction business is unique to your market, the services you offer, your operations, your experience, and the value you deliver to your customers. Don't let anyone convince you otherwise.

One way in which others will unintentionally destroy your construction business is to convince you to use the industry standards for construction. If you take nothing else away from this book, I hope you are convinced of this: there are no industry standards for the construction industry.

What are some of the commonly accepted industry standards that will drive your business into the ground?

A contractor is not supposed to charge more than 20% for overhead and profit.

Wrong. A 20% markup yields a 16.7% margin. If you have expenses of 20%, then you are making a -3.3% net profit, otherwise known as going out of business. Some healthy construction businesses could have expenses as high as 23% of total revenue. And in order to thrive, most construction businesses should be earning a 10% net profit. That's a 33% margin (23% plus 10%). A markup of 50% produces a 33% margin. Imagine telling customers your markup is 50%. They would have a conniption.

Contractors are not supposed to charge a customer for coming out to look at a job and writing up a quote.

Wrong. Construction business owners are like any other professionals. They should get paid to do work. Try calling up your doctor and ask her to come out to your house on Saturday morning before the kids' soccer games, draw your blood, take the blood back to her lab, diagnose the problem, write up a prescription, and deliver that prescription to your house. Once the prescription is presented, then you'll decide whether or not you'll pay for the doctor's time and expertise in curing your illness. Good luck with that. But the so-called industry standards state that contractors are supposed to work for free in order to earn the right to bid on a job.

Customers should get three bids in order to determine if they are getting a fair price.

Wrong. What's a fair price? Compared to what? My price might be higher because you are comparing me to another contractor who is going out of business. When customers are looking for a fair price, they are really looking for the lowest price. If customers want the lowest price, all they need to do is keep calling contractors. Eventually they will find someone incompetent or ignorant enough to give them the price they are looking for, but it won't necessarily produce the quality they are looking for.

Don't get sucked into the industry standards mantra that is repeated ad nauseum by customers who don't actually understand the industry. If your customers insist on relying on industry standards, then explain to them that the only industry standard for the construction industry is this: Most construction businesses go out of business within the first five years, and the ones that do stay in business struggle to make a sustainable profit.[4]

Educate your customers about how you are unique and sell them on your unique value. A construction business should have a simple business plan - charge an appropriate price that reflects the quality and level of service that you provide and that produces a profit for your business. That's as simple as a business plan gets.

---

[4] Shane, S. (2018). Small Business Failure Rates by Industry: The Real Numbers - Small Business Trends. [online] Small Business Trends. Available at: https://smallbiztrends.com/2012/09/failure-rates-by-sector-the-real-numbers.html [Accessed 16 Sep. 2018].

Unlike industry standards that don't exist, there are some rules of thumb that can help your construction business thrive. But before we get into those, let's review two more common problems construction businesses face when implementing the PFC system.

2. **Perfect is the enemy of good.** Some construction business owners make the mistake of trying to create and perfect a system before practicing it. They spend countless hours studying the details and methods of the plans to ensure they execute the production flawlessly. This mental fortitude serves builders in the building aspects of their work, but it can hamper them if they apply it to PFC. Mike calls it "analysis paralysis."

If you are feeling stuck by the numbers or get lost adjusting the percentages, then just move on to the next chapter. You don't need to perfect PFC the first time out. You just need it to be good enough to get started. I like how Mike puts it, "Perfectionism kills every dream - better to just start."

3. **Test before you launch.** I recently saw the trailer for *First Man* - a biopic about Neil Armstrong and the United States' mission to put the first man on the Moon. In the trailer, Neil Armstrong, played by Ryan Gosling, declares, "We need to fail. We need to fail down here so that we don't fail up there." That's exactly why you shouldn't start with the Recommended PTRs. These are the targets. You need to start with some test flights and training runs. If you have never made a profit in your business, then it will be difficult, if not impossible, to set aside 10% in profit and 10% in owner's compensation. You need to build up to that. You need to start small and work your way to the PTRs in Figure 9. Don't shoot for the moon until you've learned to fly.

If you learn to ignore the so-called industry standards, don't over analyze your PFC system at first, and start small, then you will be well on your way to joining the ranks of the fiscally elite construction companies.

Don't read the words "fiscally elite" and think that means large construction company. In my opinion and in my experience, "fiscally elite" means your construction business generates somewhere around a 10% net profit and the owners of the business receive compensation outside of the salary they are paid for working in the business. If this is the case, then my guess is that you have employees that are engaged in their work and systems in place that allow you to focus on owning the business.

Focus is the key to hitting the target. The Recommended PTRs are targets, not starting points. The PTRs in the PFC system are based on sound business practices for most construction companies and will produce the GAAP percentages listed in Figure 9.

	A	B	C	D	E	F
TOTAL INCOME	$0-$250K	$250K-$500K	$500K-$1M	$1M-$5M	$5M-$10M	$10M-$50M
COGS	72%	70%	67%	65%	65%	65%
EXPENSES	22%	22%	23%	25%	25%	20%
NET PROFIT	6%	8%	10%	10%	10%	15%

Figure 9. GAAP/PFC Recommended PTR for Healthy Construction Businesses

Aspire to move toward the recommended PTRs. Your construction business may currently have better numbers than the recommended PTRs - meaning lower COGS and expenses and higher net profits.

I congratulate you along with Mike, but as Mike says,"This does not mean you can slow things down, however. You still need to push yourself. Try to become the elite of the elite."

Profit First Basics

> The key to successful *Profit First* implementation lies in stringing together a series of many small steps in a repeating pattern. So take it easy. While you slowly start to build up your *Profit First* muscle, we are also going to get you into a simple, repeating pattern. [Business owners] typically manage their money in an erratic, noisy rhythm that causes confusion and panic. But by the end of the next chapter, we will get you into a simple rhythm that will give you clarity and control over your financials.

Rules of Thumb for a Healthy Construction Business

Earlier in this chapter I told you to forget industry standards. They don't exist. You need to take control of your construction business and operate it in a way that produces the results you want. Industry standards won't get you there, but best practices can help.

Let me make the distinction between industry standards and best practices as they apply to PFC.

Industry standards are external to your business and general in nature. Industry standards refer to "a set of criteria within an industry relating to the standard functioning and carrying out of operations in their respective fields of production."[5] Best practices are internal to your business and specific in nature. Best practices are professional procedures that are prescribed as being correct or most effective.

PFC, when fully implemented, will become the best practice for your construction business. But you don't have to wait until you have a fully implemented and fine-tuned PFC system in place. PFC can also serve as your rule of thumb.

In the early days of owning my own construction business, my drywall sub opened my eyes to the power and efficiency of rules of thumb. He told me the way he figures drywall for a normal room is to take the floor square footage and multiply by 3.5. He'd add about 10% to cover waste, and that ballpark figure got him really close. He then explained that he divided the board square footage by 32 (a 4'x8' sheet of drywall) and rounded up to get the number of sheets he needed. His method was simple and accurate enough to get a takeoff and produce a price.

You have dozens of these rules just floating around in your head. The rules of thumb that translate into best practices for the financial operations of your business exist too. Like learning about the 3.5 method for drywall was eye opening for me, these rules of thumb can help you develop your best practices.

---

[5] US Legal, Inc. (n.d.). Industrial Standards Law and Legal Definition. Retrieved September 28, 2018, from https://definitions.uslegal.com/i/industrial-standards/

The PTRs in Figure 9 are good rules of thumb.

GAAP Rules of Thumb

Net profits at or near 10% of total revenue.

This is a sign of a healthy construction business. Above 10% net profits, you are most likely very specialized in one area of construction or one type of client or project. If you are *way* above 10% net profit, like 20%, then there are some COGS or expenses missing from the P&L.

If net profits are between 6% - 8%, then things are going well, but you feel they could be better.

If net profits are 5% or lower, then cash flow is tight and you *feel* this on a regular basis.

COGS between 65% and 70% of total revenue.

If your COGS are above 70% of total revenue, then the price for the work may be too low, or the cost of labor is too high for the production output. COGS above 70% is pretty typical for a small construction business where the owner is doing most of the production work. Construction businesses of this size also suffer from a lack of confidence in pricing strategy. These business owners aren't marking up the COGS by enough to produce sustainable growth.

Expenses between 15% and 25% of total revenue.

Expenses are going to vary greatly depending on the size and scope of your construction business, but you should expect to spend between 15% to 25% of total revenue on expenses. Small construction companies and start-ups will most likely have lower expenses. These expenses will increase over time until your business reaches a point where they will flatten out.
For example, if you hire two more employees for your field operations, your COGS goes up. But so will your income because you have sold more work. But the admin staff that has to process payroll for those two additional employees doesn't necessarily

require more time. How much longer does it take to process seven payroll checks compared to five? Not much. This is a simplified example, but the point is that your expenses will flatten out over time. That doesn't mean that the dollar amount goes down. Remember we are talking percentages here.

As your company goes from $1M to $2M in total revenue, your expenses may remain near 25% of your total income. This is $250,000 for the $1M business and $500,000 for the $2M business. You may find that it doesn't take $250,000 to produce and manage another $1M worth of work. In that case your expenses will actually go down in percentage, even though the dollar amount increased.

Within these ranges are generally where you want your numbers to be as they relate to your P&L statement. Let's break these down into PFC terms, specifically, rules of thumb for your PTRs. Refer back to Figure 8 from the previous chapter (Initial Assessment for a General Contractor).

Your Net Profit Percentage of Total Revenue (Net Profit PTR)

The "real revenue" TAPs (*Profit First*) produced a translated recommended PTR of 5.91% (PFC). This is lower than the healthy 10% net profit listed above. So what gives?
Your initial assessment is a starting point for all of your PTRs. They point us in the right direction. As you move along and adjust your PTRs, you will naturally find what works for your construction business.

Profit First Basics

Perhaps you will never quite reach the TAPs [PTRs] to which you aspire. But they will force you to constantly think about what you are doing and how you are doing it, so that you can get closer. Or maybe you can beat the [PTR]s.

Maybe you can establish new best practices for your [PTR]s. That would be badass.
…at this point your PROFIT account will fund your profit distributions and serve as your rainy-day fund, you'll want your

---

FORGET INDUSTRY STANDARDS

> [PTR] to grow past 5 percent quickly. If you save 5 percent of your company's annual income, for example, that represents about twenty-one days of operating cash, which would help you keep your business afloat if your income were to plummet. (If your income dried up, you would stop contributing to your PROFIT account and TAX account and stop profit distributions to owners.) Three weeks is not much time to fix the problem, but the Armageddon rarely happens. More often, revenue slows down over time, and you'll have at least something coming in during lean times… If your sales were to stop completely, with not a single deposit coming in, here's a good longevity rule of thumb for [PTR]:
> 1. 3 percent net profit allocation = 3 weeks of operating cash
> 2. 6 percent net profit allocation = 2 months of operating cash
> 3. 12 percent net profit allocation = 5 months of operating cash.
>
> Why is it that as the profit allocation percentages basically double, business longevity almost triples? The math doesn't seem to make sense at first glance. But it does make sense. The bigger your net profit allocation percentage, the more efficiently you are running your business, which means less in operating expenses. So not only do you have more saved up with a higher Profit First percentage, you spend less, which affords you even more time.

Owner's Comp PTR

You are the most important employee in your business. Without you there is no business. Mike says, "Your business should be set up to serve you; you are not there to serve the business. Stop surviving off the leftovers."

One reason that you don't have any money is because you are not charging your clients for the value of the work that you do within the company as its most valued employee. Mike explains the importance of paying the most important employee in the business - the owner.

Profit First Basics

> Owner's Comp is the amount you and the other equity owners take in pay for the work you do. I suspect you are familiar with the term owner-operator, which means you own the business (have equity) and you operate the business (work as an employee in the business). Owner's Comp is the money we reserve for you and any other owner-operators of the business to get paid for the work you do in the business. (Equity members of your company who do not work in the business just get a profit distribution.) Your salary should be on a par with the going rate for the work you do, in other words—the salary you would have to pay your replacement.
>
> There are two options to consider when choosing your Owner's Comp [PTR] number. Either
>
> 1. Take a realistic look at the work you do. If you have a small company with, say, five employees, you may call yourself the CEO—but that's just the title on your card. It's likely you are doing a lot of other work. You probably spend a lot of time selling, completing projects, handling customers, and dealing with human resources (HR) concerns. In reality, around [20] percent of your time is spent actually doing the job of CEO: [business development, sales, estimating, project management, marketing, etc]. Determine your salary based on what you are doing 80 percent of the time, and what you would reasonably pay employees to do those jobs. Then evaluate pay for all equity owners who work in the business.
>
> Add up the salaries that represent your Owner's Comp draw. The percentage of revenue that you set as your Owner's Comp [PTR] must, at minimum, cover Owner's Comp draw…
>
> OR
> 2. Pick the percentage…in the [Initial] Assessment, based on your revenue range, [or set a target goal of 10% PTR for OWNER'S COMP]. (Refer to Figure [7].) The money that is transferred into this account is divided among all

> equity employees. It does not have to be split up equally, nor does it have to be split up based on your equity percentages.
>
> Why should you have a separate account if you and the other equity owners working in the business are just employees? Because you are the most important employee. If you had to fire people, I suspect you would fire everyone else before you fired yourself. Think about your very best employee. I'll bet you take extra steps to ensure that you are taking care of that person. I'll bet you would do everything in your power to keep your best employees happy, including paying them what they're worth, right? Well guess what! You are your best, most important employee. We must take care of you. When it comes to pay, different business formations require you to take Owner's Comp in different ways. An S Corporation is different from an LLC (limited liability company) or a sole proprietorship, which are both treated way differently than a C Corporation. The Owner's Comp allocation still works the same way; you just need to work with your accountant to make sure the money flows out properly and legally. I strongly recommend an accountant who is a certified Profit First Professional, who knows exactly how to support your Profit First business.

Mike makes it so clear and reminds me of a story about one of my clients.

I was working through a pricing strategy session with BJ. BJ is the owner operator of American Spirit Custom Builders in Tempe, AZ. BJ was taking owner's draws when he needed money to pay his personal bills. Because these were distributions (from the balance sheet) and not payroll expenses (from the P&L statement) his COGS and expenses were artificially low. He spent about forty hours a week out in the field working with his crew with the bags on and another twenty hours a week trying to run the business. The amount that he took in owner's draws was about what he would have to pay a lead carpenter for the same level of field work. But the value of the time he spent running the business, as CEO, sales person, estimator and project manager was not reflected anywhere on the books. That means that he was giving the value of the office work away for free to his clients. He never even gave his clients the opportunity to pay for the value of the work because the numbers never even showed up in any financial reports.

When we added the value of this field work as a lead carpenter into his COGS and increased the expenses to include a part-time CEO (twenty hours a week doing sales, estimating, project management, and business development), his net profit was negative.

For the first time BJ could see exactly where the money was going, and for the first time he knew exactly what he needed to charge in order to make a profit. This realization happened because the numbers don't lie. If something happened to BJ and he couldn't work, then he would need to hire not only a lead carpenter, but also a CEO.

Like most owner-operators in this scenario, BJ was booked up a few months in advance. This gave him a false sense of security. BJ explained:

> I didn't understand how we could be so busy and do such good work, but never have any money. But once I realized I needed to charge my clients for all the work that I was performing in the business, then it became clear what I needed to do. I needed to charge more for the value of the work, and I needed to find clients that were willing to pay for the value of that work.

Within a few months of implementing PFC, BJ was able to start setting aside profits, pricing future work that would not only pay him for the field work he and his crews produced but also pay him for the value of the work he did in running the business. He generated profits and gave himself a raise at the same time. He went from scraping by, to paying himself in three ways. He paid himself as a lead carpenter (from COGS), as the CEO (from the expenses), and as an owner (from the net profits).

The bottom line is this: you have to charge your clients for the value of all the work that your company produces in order pay for your expenses (your salary as a CEO) and generate a net profit (your distribution as an owner). For the owner-operator, you must get paid for all the work you do - as labor in the COGS, as the CEO in the expenses, and as the owner in the distribution of net profits.

Like I said before, you don't *have to* pay yourself in any of these ways and you'll still show up for work tomorrow. But you don't *have to* give this value away to your customers, either. The right clients want to pay for this value because the service that comes along with it is extraordinary.

Your Tax PTR

You met Jayme Martin and his wife, Sarah, in the introduction of this book. Jayme was trapped in the craftsman cycle and never had enough money to pay himself or his bills on a regular basis. He kept feeding the beast, robbing Peter to pay Paul, by booking more work to keep money coming in. Pay himself? Not possible. Paying his taxes on time? Ha! Who can do that?

Jayme finally had enough, and we started working his PFC plan. He raised his prices in order to cover his expenses and yield a small net profit. He started saying "No" to the wrong clients. (He "Pumpkin Planned" them.) And he set up his bank accounts. He started small. Within six months, he had cash. Real money sitting in a bank account designated as TAX. At the end of the first quarter of 2018 he sent the government its money because it was there ready to go.

No one loves taxes, but they are a fact of life. One way to get enjoyment out of this civic responsibility is to eliminate the pain. The government is going to get its money, but they don't need to steal the joy of running a healthy construction business, too.

According to Mike, "[This] is not about accounting to the exact penny. That's what your bookkeeper and accountant do." You don't have an accountant or bookkeeper? Get one. A good one. When you start implementing PFC you are going to be able to focus more of your time and energy generating profitable projects for your business. You don't need to spend time producing financial reports. You can hire someone to do that. And you'll be able to pay them less than what you can earn for the business when you focus on that. So, get a good bookkeeper and CPA now!

Where was I? Oh yeah, the exact penny.

There is one reason that the US tax code is tens of thousands of pages long. It's complicated. PFC is going to simplify the process for you. We allocate cash based on PTRs and serve it up to the "small plate bank accounts."

Profit First Basics

> The Tax plate, so we are clear, is designed to pay the direct Tax liabilities of the business and (this is the big one), the personal income taxes of the owners. Let me say that again because this often gets missed: your company (assuming you own it) will reserve your personal income tax liability for you, and then pay it. Here's the deal: you started your business in part to achieve financial freedom. So if that is true, shouldn't your company pay your taxes for you? ...So that is exactly what is going to happen.
>
> When your taxes are due and you submit your quarterlies, the company will send the payment in for you. Don't get stuck in the micro details here. This system always works if you have taxes drawn from your paycheck (maybe you don't take distributions as you would from an LLC, but take a paycheck from an S-Corp or a C-Corp), then the company will reimburse you for your taxes. All taxes (including, scratch that, especially yours) are paid by your business, not you. Got it? Good.
>
> The first step in getting to your Tax [PTR] is to determine your income tax rate. Taxes range all over the place, depending on your amount of personal income and corporate profit and the area you live in. As of this writing, many entrepreneurs have an average income tax rate of 35 percent or so; for others it will be less, and in some countries it can be 60 percent or more.
>
> One goal of the Profit First system is that the company takes care of all forms of Tax responsibility. It's mandatory that you talk with your accountant so she can advise you on all the ways you and your business will be taxed.

NOTE: *Profit First* recommends you do this approach and use real revenue instead of total revenue to determine this percentage. That may be more accurate because your tax liability will be based on your profit (meaning after expenses are deducted from the total revenue), but the dollar amount of materials and subcontractors may vary from job to job. PFC uses PTR to simplify the system.

Three Simple Approaches to Determining Your Tax PTR

Let's make one of the most complicated aspects of you financial super-simple – determining your tax PTR. Here are three ways to calculate it:

1. Break out your tax returns - the personal and business.

> Add up your taxes and then determine the percentage of taxes you paid compared to your [total] Revenue. Do this again for the prior two years. Looking at your taxes as a percentage of [total] Revenue for the last three years will give you a good sense of your ongoing tax responsibility

If you had a total revenue of $1,000,000 last year, paid yourself $100,000 in salary, and generated net profits of $100,000, then you might have the following tax liability for you and the business:

Personal Tax Liability = $100,000 x 25% Effective Tax Rate = $25,000

Business Tax Liability = $100,000 x 35% Corporate Tax Rate = $35,000

Total Tax Liability = $25,000 + $35,000 = $60,000

Right now, there are CPAs out their rolling their eyes and saying, "That's not how you calculate personal or corporate tax liability. It's more complicated than that." Yes, I know, and that's the point. It is complicated. You need a simplified system to be accurate enough to ease your pain.

If your total revenue was $1,000,000 last year and you had a total tax liability of $60,000 then your tax PTR is 6% ($60,000 / $1,000,000).

When you receive your next progress payment for a job, you'll know that 6% of that check is not yours; it's the government's money.

And what happens if you do $2,000,000 worth of work next year. Well, I will assume it's because you are implementing PFC and growing your business in a profitable way, so you will be making profits more efficiently. That means making more profits with less spending. That will translate to a higher tax bill. So you may need to bump up your tax PTR from 6% to 7% or even 8% to make sure you are covered.

Keep it simple. You make the profits and put some aside based on what you've done in the past. Let your accountant do the complicated stuff. That's why you hired her.

2. Get your estimated tax responsibility for your business from your CPA for the year to date (YTD) and then determine your tax PTR YTD. That's a lot of abbreviations. Sorry about that.

3. Use a tax PTR of 6% to get started. Trust me. You need at least this much for your taxes.

Now that you have clear picture of the financial landscape of your construction business, you are ready to get started on the journey. The next chapter will show you how to walk through your first year of PFC and give you the proven strategies that will guide you to the promised land of profits.

Before we close out this chapter, let's summarize the rules of thumbs we've covered here and use these to perform the action steps at the end of this chapter.

Rules of Thumb for PFC

GAAP percentages of total revenue for a healthy construction business:

COGS: 65% - 70%
Expenses: 15% - 25%
Net profit: 8% - 10%

The categories above will show up on your P&L statement.

PFC PTRs for a healthy construction business:

Tax: 6% - 10%
Owner's comp: 10% -15%
Net profit: 8% - 10%
Total OPEX: 76% - 65%

The categories above are defined by your PFC system. Refer to the Glossary of Terms in the Appendix to see the relationship between the GAAP terms and the PFC terms. Your PRT allocations will be based on these numbers.

Action Steps:

Design your construction business for profits by determining your PTRs. You might be lost in all the numbers and a little confused as to how we got here. Let's make these action steps super-simple and use the rules of thumb as a starting point.

1. Profit account: Set your profit PTR at 1%. If you are able to set it higher based your initial assessment, then great. Do it. But there's no need to start out of the gate that fast. You'll get there. More on this in the next chapter.

2. Owner's comp: Ask yourself, "How much would I have to pay an employee with my level of skills and abilities to perform the work I do in the field?" Then ask yourself, "How much would I have to pay an employee that could walk in here on day one and do estimating, design, marketing, project management, sales, business development, and the other seventeen jobs I do when I am not in the field?" The answers to these questions should inform you as to what you should be paying yourself for the value of the work you do in the business. You probably can't pay yourself this, but again, this would be a target to hit.

Calculate the total compensation for all the owners of the business if they performed work in the business. Now divide that number by your total revenue and multiply by 100%. Is owner's comp near 10%? If not, then that would be my first goal. More on this in the next chapter. For now, just do the calculation.

3. Tax account: Like you did with owner's comp, calculate the total amount in taxes you paid last year, including the owners' personal taxes. Remember the business is here to serve the owner(s), and part of that service is paying for the taxes generated when the owner(s) makes a profit. Take the total tax paid and divide by the total revenue and multiply by 100%. This is a good place to start for your tax PTR allocation. In the next chapter we will discuss how and when to increase this number. For now, just do the calculation.

4. Total OPEX: This is the big one. Once you have set aside your profits, paid yourself from the owner's comp account, and paid your taxes, then all you have remaining are the leftovers. You have to operate your business off of this amount. As painful as this might seem right now, it will get better. You are looking at your construction business with polarized lenses. You can see the details below the surface.

Take the PTRs you calculated in the steps above and subtract them from 100%. This is your PTR for total OPEX. Don't worry about how high this number is right now. In the next chapter we are going to start putting the plan together to decrease this number. For now, just do the calculation.

Calculating these PTRs is burning calories, trimming the fat. Your construction business is on the way to becoming a lean, mean cash-generating machine. (Cue the *Rocky* theme music.)

Chapter 8

RIPPING OFF THE BAND-AID

I could feel the stress through the phone the first time I spoke with Jason Mollak. You first met Jason in Chapter 1. He is the contractor from Omaha who celebrated his success in Profit First for Contractors by taking his wife on a vacation for the first time in eleven years.

"Shawn, I don't know what I am going to do. I feel like I messed up, and I don't know how to fix it," Jason told me on our first phone call.

I listened intently as Jason described the situation that was about to put him out of business.

"The GC on this big job owes me [tens of thousands of dollars] and said that I will get paid when he gets paid. But it's been sixty days, and he still doesn't have the money. What should I do?" Jason asked.

"Do you have any money?" I asked.

"No," Jason responded with what seemed to be shame in his voice.

"Can you get any money?" I asked.

"No. We just finished building a new house, and all our money is tied up there," he told me.

"Ok. If the contractor doesn't have the money, then you need to go to the person that does. And you need to do this tomorrow." Over the next forty-five minutes we formulated Plan A and Plan B. Then we came up with contingencies for each of those plans and contingencies to the contingencies.

Admitting you need help is a lonely, painful ordeal. Digging into the underlying issues often hurts. The Initial Assessment can hurt. Trying to dial in your PTRs and figure out how to make the numbers work can be a painful process.

Exposing your numbers in this way is like getting a financial colonoscopy.

Speaking of colonoscopies (nice segue, Shawn), they used to be a painful and sometimes lengthy process. Nowadays, they just knock you out, do the procedure, and wake you up. Thank God for modern medicine. But there is something we can learn from colonoscopies that will help you through what might be a painful process right now.

In an article about first impressions, Daniel McCarthy discusses the groundbreaking work of Daniel Kahneman, a Nobel Prize winning economist and author of the book, *Thinking Fast and Slow*. It turns out that after a painful colonoscopy treatment, patients would forget about the overall duration of the pain they experienced and would instead remember their experience based on the peak moments of pain and on how it ended. McCarthy explains that Kahneman discovered:

> A patient whose colonoscopy lasted an agonizing 25 minutes, for example (Patient B), would rate the experience better and would happily come back a year later for his follow-up appointment, as long as the treatment ended with less pain. Another patient (Patient A), who only had around 8 minutes of total pain, wouldn't come back next year because he remembers the pain of how the experience ended.[6]

What does that have to do with PFC?

If we ended the book now, after the initial assessment and the number crunching – the peak pain – and sent you out into the world to implement PFC, you may not come back because you will remember the way it ended. But, according to Kahneman's

---

[6] McCarthy, J. (2018). Why First Impressions Don't Matter Much. [online] The Psychology of Wellbeing. Available at: http://psychologyofwellbeing.com/201204/why-first-impressions-dont-matter-much.html [Accessed 17 Sep. 2018].

research, your experience depends on the peak moments of pain and how it ends, more than the duration.

It's the classic debate: Is it better to rip off the band-aid quickly in one quick tug, or slowly with care and some deep breathing. The peak pain may be the same, but according to research the way something ends is what you will remember, even if the duration is longer.

If you are feeling pain at that this point, that's because we just ripped off the band-aid. Although the pain of the initial assessment might have been intense for you, I want to make sure that this procedure ends in a positive way. Whether you are a "just rip it off and get it over with" or a "please, go slowly" person, this chapter is designed to give you a plan for finishing well.

But before you can finish the journey, you need to start. That's what happened with that first phone call with Jason. We put together a plan to get the money he was owed. He stopped the bleeding. After that he worked very, very hard at changing key aspects of his business.

I recently asked Jason what PFC did for him. He responded:

> I am able to spend more time with my family and the fear of the unknown is gone. I can finally take a vacation. [Because of Profit First] I know where the money is. There are no questions. It is either there, or it's not. There's less weight on my shoulders. The risk of overspending is gone. This was a huge relief for my wife. She felt all the pain and the stress, too. But now it's gone. This was a huge accomplishment for us. I take my work seriously as a craftsman. But my job as a father and husband, I take even more seriously. That is the legacy I am building.

Well done, Jason. I am proud of you.

Let's start working your plan so you can feel proud of the legacy you are building.

The Problem with CPAs

I am most likely going to offend many CPAs with this section of the book, but I don't care about them. They will be fine. I care about you - the construction business owner. I want you to have a profitable construction business. Much of the advice you get from your CPAs may be technically correct in terms of limiting or determining your tax liabilities, but the service you get from your CPA is costing you more money than it's saving you in taxes.

Your CPA has one job - to help you determine your tax liability. Good CPAs will tell you how to limit your tax liabilities. Great CPAs will help you make more profits. Many CPAs take the information you give them, plug it into the appropriate tax forms, and then tell you how much you owe the government.

The reason many CPAs cost you money, as opposed to making you money, is that they don't sell you services beyond filing your tax return. You think that your CPA is reviewing the overall financial state of your business and helping you run your business better. But the truth is that you sent your CPA a bunch of transactional information in the form of receipts, invoices, and bank statements and a few weeks or months later they send you back some forms to sign and the bill due to Uncle Sam. Ouch. That's a painful end to the procedure.

Your CPA can only be as good at helping with your business as you are at running your business.

Your CPA works for you. If you want your CPA to make you money instead of costing you money, then you have to direct the CPA's work. In order to do that, your CPA must understand how a construction business makes money. If your CPA can't explain to you how a construction business makes a profit, then find a CPA who can.

It's your business. You are responsible for it. You CPA is not. It's up to you.

Here are a few examples of CPA advice that cost you money:

Pay yourself through owner's draws. This is the most common mistake that I see. Depending on the legal structure of the business, this is one way to limit your tax liability. But as we discussed in Chapter 2, owner's distributions (draws) should occur only when the business is profitable. Owner's draws do not show up on the P&L statement. Technically taking an owner's draw may save you some money in taxes, but it's costing you more in lost revenues because you are not pricing your work correctly. Your COGS and expenses are artificially suppressed. You'll never make a net profit if the net profit at the bottom of the P&L statement isn't correct.

Spend money in order to reduce your tax liability. Again, this is technically correct. If you increase your expenses, then you will be taxed on less. But if you aren't making a profit, should you be spending more? "Buy a new $35,000 truck and you'll save on your taxes." Do you have $35,000 for a truck or do you know how an expense like that makes you money? Probably not. I am all about spending money on tools, equipment, and people, for that matter, that can make you money. Spending cash you don't have on unplanned expenses in order to save a few bucks on taxes is not wise.

Send me over your files and I will work on them. You're probably familiar with the phrase "garbage in, garbage out." What happens if you don't send all the information your CPA needs to accurately file your taxes? Most decent CPAs will give you a list of information they need in order to complete your tax filings. But reading through this list might as well be like trying to decipher hieroglyphics. Just because a CPA is a CPA does not mean that she is a business person. Watch out for CPAs who don't help you organize your financial business documents. I have seen many contractors held hostage by their CPAs. I put the responsibility of the financial organization of the business on the business owner, but great CPAs will help you organize your information. This is an additional service that you should request. Remember, the primary service a CPA offers is tax filing, not business consulting. Look for a CPA who is willing to sell you additional consulting services that grow your profits. As you become more profitable through PFC, you'll need to know how to make the best use of your money.

As Mike says in *Profit First*:

> Most accountants using the old GAAP method of cash management are lucky to have a handful of profitable clients. Almost all of the remaining clients are likely struggling to stay afloat. This should be their wake-up call.
>
> Ask your [CPA] to read *Profit First* cover to cover and support you in the process. If they are unwilling to listen to you (remember, you are the client, and their job is specifically to support you in maximizing your profitability), find new accounting professionals who not only support *Profit First* but are trained in it. (If you don't know where to start, check out ProfitFirstProfessionals.com.)

During the 12 months I spent training to become a certified Profit First Professional (PFP), I met Shanna (pronounced Shaw-na, not Shay-na) Quinn. I was looking for a PFP that would serve my clients in their day-to-day bookkeeping needs as well as help them with their PFC journey. Shanna was a godsend.

Shanna's father was a general contractor and she understood how construction companies make money. She joined PFP in 2017, and that's when I started referring my clients to Shanna for their bookkeeping needs. Most accounting professionals have never heard of Profit First, and many, when they do, don't get it. It goes against everything they learned (GAAP). That's why working with Shanna is so refreshing. Shanna told me, "I have always wanted to do more for my clients than just manage their bank feed and reconcile their accounts. I wanted to serve a niche with my business and I have always admired the work contractors do because of my dad."

I have clients all over the world and Shanna is located in Florida. She serves many of my US-based clients better than their previous bookkeepers that were in the same town. Many of my clients never realized that their bookkeeper could be in another time zone, but they are thrilled with Shanna and the peace of mind she creates for them.

Your financial people (CPA and bookkeeper) need to be on board with PFC. If they will not get on board, find someone who will. Just realize that person may not be in your town.

Getting from Here to There

In 1959, a North Carolina newspaper published a cartoon panel that depicted an aircraft mid-flight. The joke that accompanied the illustration went like this:

> A conscientious airplane pilot addressed his passengers over the intercommunication system, telling them that he had lost his way. He explained that the radar was not working, the radio beam could not be picked up, and the compass was broken. "But," he added encouragingly, "you will be glad to know that we're making very good time."[7]

When you're lost, speed is not your friend.

The same applies to implementing PFC. You're reading this book because you needed a course correction for your business. Your compass was broken and your radar was on the fritz, but you were going at top speed.

Now it's time to slow the pace to ensure that you arrive at the destination you set out to reach when you started your business - profitability and sustainable growth. The work you have done over the last couple chapters probably revealed a gap between where you are now (the initial assessment) and where you want to be (recommended PTRs).

This gap is common. This gap is scary, but this gap is manageable. The remainder of this chapter is going to give you the steps to follow so that you avoid trying to leap over this gap like some kind of super-preneur (I made that word up. It means super entrepreneur). But instead we are going to fill in the gap with terra firma (I didn't make those words up. They're Latin. They mean firm land. I had to look it look up.)

---

[7] Quoteinvestigator.com. (2018). We're Lost, But We're Making Good Time! – Quote Investigator. [online] Available at: https://quoteinvestigator.com/2012/07/11/making-good-time/ [Accessed 17 Sep. 2018].

Be Hungry - Cut Expenses

When my wife announced that we were going to have a lifestyle change and follow the Whole30 nutrition plan, we started researching the foods we could eat and those we couldn't. We tested out recipes and got rid of the junk food. The key to our success is that we employed these strategies *before* we started the 30 days.

In the weeks leading up to going cold turkey (you can actually eat lots of cold turkey as long as it is organic with no additives), I increasingly became more and more hungry. I wanted to eat all the time. But the interesting thing about adjusting to this change in our diet is that I could eat all the time…as long as I ate the right things. My relationship with food changed. I no longer craved food. Food was just fuel. I needed fuel because my body was changing. My hunger made me very aware of when I needed to eat and how food made me feel.

PFC is not a diet - something you apply to your business to shed a few inefficiencies and tone up your flabby operations. PFC is a complete nutrition plan for your business. Profit, taxes, owner's compensation, and operating expenditures are the fuel for your business. Viewing the income for your business through the polarized lenses of PFC will make you hungry, but hungry in a good way. You'll have the motivation you need to cut out all the junk, all the expenses that are draining your profits.
You are going to be hungry, but when you cut out unnecessary expenses, you're going to feel better.

Trim Fat - Don't Cut Out the Muscle

In the process of cutting expenses, don't make the mistake that many health-nuts make. Mike says, "You want to cut the fat out of your business,…but you don't want to cut out the muscle. For example, you might decide that your books are a mess because you have been DIY-ing them for so long. You get on the PFC train and decide, "I have to cut expenses. I can't afford a professional bookkeeper." This would be cutting muscle. Let a professional bookkeeper do the heavy lifting.

The same philosophy holds with other people you pay for services. Spend the money on an expert subcontractor who might charge more but allows you to deliver a project with higher quality and in less time. Ditch the guy that is costing you time and quality. You know the one(s) I am talking about…the subcontractor that you have to babysit. In fact, give him your copy of PFC when you're done.

You should review every line item in your expenses every month and make sure they are in line with your budget. If your meals and entertainment budget is $250 each month, and you spend $300, adjust the budget for the following month to $200. Better yet, do business at the coffee shop instead of the steakhouse. Slash that line item. Trim that fat.

Don't cut the bookkeeper and the expert subcontractor. Hire them. That's the muscle. You'll need that muscle for the next step.

Raise Your Prices

Cutting expenses is one way to increase margins. Doing more with less encourages you to innovate. You should always be looking for ways to limit your expenses and making sure you are getting your highest level of performance out of your COGS.

When I work through an initial assessment and a pricing strategy session with my clients and we adjust the COGS to reflect the actual dollars being spent on COGS, the actual PTR for the COGS is almost always too high (above 70% of total revenue).

I will then ask my clients, "How can you reduce your COGS?" This question is always met with silence. Their minds are racing, and I know what they are thinking, "Is he asking me who I should fire?"

After a few seconds of tense reflection, I put them at ease. "One way to reduce your COGS is to tell John you are working with a business coach and he said that you have to cut costs. This means that you are going to have to pay John $20 per hour instead of his current wage of $25. What is John going to say?" My clients usually respond with something like, "Yeah. John will quit."

And we don't want John to quit. We like John. He's a good employee and he does good work. Cutting John's pay, although it would reduce the labor portion of the COGS, won't solve the problem.

It is the ratio of COGS to total revenue that is too high, not necessarily the dollar amount of COGS. One way to reduce this ratio is to sell the COGS for a higher price. When you divide a number by a bigger number, the value of that fraction decreases.

If your COGS is $700,000 and your total revenue is $1,000,000, the PTR of the COGS sold is 70%.

$700,000 (COGS) / $1,000,000 (PRICE) x 100% = 70%

If you sold the same amount of work for a higher price, then the PTR of the COGS would go down.

If your COGS is $700,000 and your total revenue is $1,100,000 (because you raised your prices), then the PTR of the COGS would be:

$700,000 (COGS) / $1,100,000 (PRICE) x 100% = 63.6%

Do the same amount of work, just charge more for it.

"But Shawn I can't just raise my prices. My clients won't pay higher prices."

I know your existing clients won't. That's why we need to get you better clients. Better clients are going to pay higher prices. They have to if they want you to stay in business and make a profit.

Cutting expenses will help get your business lean and mean and will increase the bottom line. And hear this again: you have to review your expenses each month and get fired up about setting a budget and sticking to it.

Raising prices without raising expenditures will fast track your success with PFC.

"But Shawn, I'm scared to raise my prices."

I understand, but think of it this way: Once you realize that your salary is either a COGS or expense (or a combination of the two), and you take it into account on your P&L statement, you determine the markup you need to make a profit. You aren't really raising your price. You are being more accurate with your COGS and expenses.

Remember this equation from Chapter 2:

PRICE = COSTS x MARKUP FACTOR

When you determine your actual COGS and apply a markup factor to those COGS, you calculate your price. The more accurate you are at determining your COGS, the more accurate your markup factor will be.

What you were charging before was a guess. Now you can charge what you need to pay for your expenses and make a net profit. And when you hear that your price is high, you must ask "Compared to what?"

The client's budget?

Clients budgets are always too low. Never in the history of construction has a client had a budget that is too high for the work she wants done.

Other construction companies?

Of course, you're higher than they are. They are most likely not charging enough to generate a profit and the owners aren't paying themselves a regular salary.

Other types of businesses?

When was the last time you were able to eat at a restaurant and tell the owner what you're willing to pay for the food. How about your doctor? Can you tell her that her prices are too high? I could go on and on, but we need to finish this chapter.

126 PROFIT FIRST FOR CONTRACTORS

Increasing your margins over time by raising prices and cutting expenses creates a lean construction company. If you want to take this lean organization to the next level, then you should also fire some of your clients. That's a subject for another book. In fact, Mike already wrote that book. It's called *The Pumpkin Plan*. You should read it after you finish this book.

Start the Journey Today

There's an old Chinese proverb that says, "The best time to plant a tree was twenty years ago. The second-best time is today."

If you don't have a tree that is producing fruit, then let's get started on planting that today.

The rest of this chapter is going to walk you through what you need to do today, this month, this quarter and this year to establish PFC in your business.

Day One:

1. Tell your financial people, your CPA, your bookkeeper, about PFC. You don't have financial people? Go get them. It's not as expensive as you think, and it will allow you to focus on running the business, not guessing at the numbers. If your financial people aren't on board with PFC – and there may be some resistance – give them a copy of this book and ask them to read it cover to cover. If they still aren't on board, then find someone else. They work for you, not the other way around.

2. Set up your bank accounts at your primary bank (income, profit, tax, owner's comp, and total OPEX). What do you mean you don't have these set up yet?! Stop what you're doing and do it now. No. You can't track PFC in a spreadsheet and you certainly can't track it in your head. Set up these accounts now!

3. Once you have your accounts set up, give them each a nickname so you can easily identify them when you log into your bank. They should look like this:

INCOME	*8855
PROFIT	*8237
TAX	*8754
OWNCOMP	*8823
TOTAL OPEX	*8772

4. Establish current percentages of total revenue (CPTRs). The initial assessment helped establish your recommended PTRs and the rules of thumb should have helped you see where you need to be, but the Recommended PTRs are the target, not the starting point. You need to start this journey with a single step - a small step. As Mike states:

> We're going to start with a manageable profit, a doable Owner's Comp, and a reasonable Tax reserve that will allow adequate time to cut down on [expenditures], start finding profit opportunities within your business, and adjust to the new system. The percentages we are about to assign to each account are going to be called your [CPTRs (current percentages of Total Revenue)]. For your [CPTR]s, we'll start at our Day Zero* contribution levels for each account and then add 1%, bringing us to Day One* of your [PFC] implementation. This may mean your Day Zero is zilch for a few of the accounts. If your business has never had a profit, or if you have sometimes had a profit and sometimes a loss, your profit has been zero. Therefore, our easy Day One start for the PROFIT account will be 1% [PTR] (that's 0% historically plus 1%, starting today), and we will bump it up as we start getting into our quarterly rhythm.

	DAY ONE	QRT 1	QRT 2	QRT 3	QRT 4
NET PROFIT	1%	2%	4%	6%	8%
OWNER'S COMP	10%	10%	10%	10%	8%
TAX	6%	7%	7%	8%	8%
TOTAL OPEX	83%	81%	79%	76%	76%

Figure 10. Day One PTR

Profit First Basics

> If your company historically has paid taxes of 5 percent of your total revenue, we are going to set up your tax [CPTR] reserve at 6 percent by simply adding 1 percent to your Day Zero tax allocation of 5 percent. If your pay represented 9 percent of your income, we add 1 percent to your 9 percent and you have 10 percent Owner Compensation [CPTR]. And so on. Even if our targets are much higher, we start with what we've got, plus 1 percent for Profit, Owner's Comp, and Tax. We then reduce the [TOTAL OPEX] by the cumulative of the percentage adjustments we made to the other three accounts.
>
> Why start with small percentages, when we likely could do more? The primary goal here is to establish a new automatic routine for you. I want the amounts to be so small you don't even feel them. The goal is to set up these automatic allocations immediately, and then adjust the percentages each quarter until we are aligned with our target distribution percentages. Take small easy steps and you will gain powerful momentum.

Start slow. Real slow. Make the goals so small it is impossible to fail. Like starting a habit of flossing - commit to flossing one tooth.

Now let's review how Mike explains managing your owner's comp percentages going forward.

> The starting [PTRs] you set are your quarterly allocation percentages. We are going to use them for the rest of this quarter, whether the quarter begins next week or in ninety-one days. Most businesses have never taken a profit before and just pay the owner as close to a regular salary as possible. In this case, Day Zero Profit will be 0 percent. Don't get upset about that; most companies have no historical profit. You are among friends here. In other cases, owners take money out of the business whenever there is any sitting around and they aren't sure whether those dollars are considered Owner's Comp or Profit. The answer is simple: all of it is Owner's Comp and none of it is profit. In this case, your Day Zero profit percentage is 0 percent. Then there are circumstances where your income statement says there is a profit, but you only took money out to

support your personal lifestyle as best you could. For our purposes, this is again a situation of no profit. Set Day Zero Profit to 0 percent. Your Day Zero Owner's Comp is the pay that you received from the company this year, either in pay checks or distributions and has not been classified as profit already (as I explained in the prior paragraph).

And just so we are clear, you likely had no profit, so the Owner's Comp will be all the pay you took.

If you are still a little unclear on what goes to Profit and what goes to Owner's Comp, simply do this: put 0 percent to Profit and put any money you (and any other owners of the business) have received into the category of Owner's Comp and figure out the historical percentage of [Total] Revenue. [You should have done this at the end of the last chapter]. By the way, if you look at the income tax returns for each owner in your business, you can find the Owner's Comp there. Just add it up.

Your day zero Tax is the amount of Tax that your business (not you personally) has paid in taxes. Has your company paid taxes directly to the government? Yes? Then add up that amount. Has the company paid the government directly for taxes on your behalf? Meaning did you get a tax bill for personal income, and then have the company write out a check to pay it? Yes? Then add that in. But did you get distributions or paychecks from your company, and then pay the tax man out of your own pocket? In that case, you paid your own income taxes and your business did not, and you would not add this into your calculation. In most cases, businesses have never paid taxes on behalf of their owners (even though they should), so the calculation here is easy. You put the day zero taxes to 0 percent, or possibly a very low percentage to account for the corporate taxes paid.

The norm for most businesses, and therefore yours, I suspect, is that the business neither paid a profit to the Owner's Comp nor paid taxes on its behalf. So in this case, we set profit to 0 percent and tax to 0 percent and Owner's Comp to the total payments to the Owner's Comp, divided by Total Revenue. And if this totally confuses you, do not worry at all. The Profit First system is self-correcting. Just set Profit and Tax historical to 0

> percent and figure out the percentage for Owner's Comp.
>
> The Operating [Expenditures] historical percentage is everything else.

Let's recall from Chapter 4 what PFC calls total OPEX. Here's the formula:

TOTAL OPEX in % =

PTR of Expenses + PTR of COGS - PTR of Owner's Comp

Mike reminds us from *Profit First*:

> These numbers do not need to be perfect. If you are the accounting type, you are going to want to get this figured out to the penny. But that is not necessary, not possible, and not even helpful. The goal here is to get to a rough starting point. The Profit First system is designed to just get started now—that's the primary goal—and will, over time, be tweaked and adjusted to get to the perfect percentages.

When you start out, your day zero percentages may look like this:

INCOME	*8855	100%
PROFIT	*8237	0%
TAX	*8754	0%
OWNCOMP	*8823	8%
TOTAL OPEX	*8772	92%

If your percentages look like this, then your company has had no historical profit, paid the owner eight percent of the total revenue, and ninety-two cents of every dollar went to pay bills.

The reason PFC is self-correcting is that the PTRs always have to add up to be 100%. If they are more than 100%, then you are spending more than you take in. This is quite common for most construction businesses. One of the main reasons for the shortfall is that your P&L might show a positive number at the bottom of the page, but your P&L doesn't account for all the money that goes out of the business (GAAP confusion). The P&L tracks the income that comes into the business over a given period of time, but it doesn't track all the money that goes out during that same time period. Huh? Why not? Because GAAP doesn't ensure profitability, it only tracks the money. And it does this with the use of the balance sheet and the P&L. When you take an owner's draw, you are taking money from the balance sheet. That's fine as long as you understand that you could be taking that money from previous earnings, not current operations. PFC forces you to look at the money in your business as it actually is - incoming and outgoing.

Your total revenue represents 100% of your budget for any given time period. If the outflow of money exceeds your income, you have no profit. That's why you have to consider owner's draws, taxes, and other outflows of money that don't show up on the P&L. The incoming dollars (total revenue) are all you have to spend on your business for that given period of time. And the incoming dollars are shown on the P&L statement.

I will say it again. Your total revenue is all the money you have to spend. It represents 100% of incoming dollars. You want your business to run on a percentage less than 100% of the total dollars available. When you do this, after all bills are paid, including taxes, then you have a profit.

CPAs have various terms for this, like net profit before taxes and net profits after taxes.

But if you show a positive net profit on the P&L and then you have to deduct the amount the owner was paid and the taxes that the company has paid, you could have a positive *net profit before taxes* and negative *net profit after taxes*.

Confusing? You bet. That's why we need to view your income for what it is - the maximum amount of money you have to spend. And we need to account for all the money that is spent in your business regardless of where that money shows up in our accounting system.

PFC is the lens, the filter, through which we view the money, the cash, the lifeblood of your business. When you have a corrected view of your money and you have a system to generate profits, then and only then will the GAAP reports make sense.

Most construction business owners, business owners in general, don't understand the way this part of the business works. Your numbers (the PTRs) are probably messed up. This is totally normal. But now it's time to throw normality out the window and start to be different. And by different, I mean profitable.

Putting Profit First into Motion

Here's how Mike recommends getting started: "Now that we know your Day Zero percentages, we are going to ease into *Profit First*. To do this, simply add 1 percent to your Day Zero Profit, 1 percent to your Owner's Comp, and 1 percent to your Tax, and reduce your [OPEX] by 3 percent. Hopefully, you see the immediate implications on your business." If we apply this small start to the day one PTR table in this chapter, then the changes required are quite clear.

Let's assume this construction business had a $1,000,000 total revenue. The day zero allocations are:

INCOME	100%	$1,000,000
PROFIT	0%	$0
TAX	0%	$0*
OWNCOMP	8%	$80,000
TOTAL OPEX	92%	$920,000

*The day zero tax allocation doesn't mean that you didn't pay taxes. You most certainly did. It means that you weren't setting aside this money, so it's zero for day zero. (If you didn't pay taxes, then you might want to get ready for a visit from the tax man.) The amount you paid in tax is mixed in with the 92% of total OPEX.

After we adjust the day zero allocation to the day one allocations, the numbers would look like this:

INCOME	100%	$1,000,000
TAX	1%	$10,000
PROFIT	1%	$10,000
OWNCOMP	9%	$90,000
TOTAL OPEX	89%	$890,000

These dollar amounts show us that we need to get the same amount of work done (total OPEX) for $890,000 instead of $920,000. Thirty thousand dollars is a lot of money, but it's only 3% less than before. When you start looking for something as small as 3% inefficiencies in production or operations, you will find it. That's why it's so important to track and scrutinize your expenditures monthly. You could also make a 3% adjustment in price. That means that what you previously sold for $100,000 you will now sell at $103,000. If your customer won't buy from you at $103,000, he was never going to buy from you at $100,000. Look for ways to increase your efficiencies and your price and you will fast track your PFC success.

5. Make your first allocation and let's make your business profitable right now. Follow this procedure from *Profit First*.

Profit First Basics

This very moment we will make a profit for your business, and we will be profitable every day going forward. Please don't just read this and then move on to the next chapter. I want you to take action now.

Right now, this moment, look at your bank balance in your original primary account, which we have renamed your OPEX account. Then subtract any outstanding checks and payments you have from that account. Transfer the remainder of the money into your INCOME account. Now we are going to do our first allocation. Divide up the money in the INCOME account to

> all the other accounts (PROFIT, OWNER'S COMP, TAX, and OPEX) based on the [CPTR]s you set. This is your first-ever "allocation" and will be the only thing you ever do with the INCOME account, besides receiving future deposits from sales.
>
> Let's do the allocation right now. Say you had $5,000 in your old primary bank account. You have renamed that account OPEX and determined that you have $3,000 in checks and payments still waiting to clear. That means you have $2,000 currently available. Transfer the $2,000 to the INCOME account. Then transfer all the money from the INCOME account to the respective accounts based on percentages.
> Run your percentages on that $2,000 and move that money into the accounts.

Here's how the allocations of that $2,000 will look in your PFC accounts:

INCOME	100% - This account which had the $2,000 goes to $0 as all the money gets allocated to profit, owner's comp, tax, and total OPEX, based upon the CPTRs we have set.
PROFIT	1% (Recommend PTR 10%) $20 goes here.
TAX	1% (Recommend PTR 6%) $20 goes here
OWNCOMP	9% (Recommend PTR 10%) $180 goes here
TOTAL OPEX	89% (Recommend PTR 74%) $1,780 goes here

Although the numbers might not be pretty, when you see them allocated in this way, you can see exactly where the money is going. In this example, a huge portion of the income is going to expenditures. At this point you may feel a little happy and sad. You feel happy because you have a system that you can understand, but you feel sad because your numbers are a bit, well, ugly. That's ok. Let's look to Mike for a pick-me-up.

Profit First Basics

> It feels good to now have a system and have clarity, but the immediate picture is ugly. And that is kind of what we want because over time you will be motivated to make the allocation percentages better and better. You will be motivated to reduce expenses, and perhaps even more important, you will find ways to increase your profitability (via innovations, thinking up new, better, and more efficient steps). This system will make it undeniably clear on what money you have and what purpose it is being used for. And with this clarity, you can make much better decisions to improve the health of your business.

Now that you've seen an example, let's make you profitable. Deposit any checks you have in your bank today. Distribute the money to all the other accounts (you may have to wait until the funds are available). Do this for every deposit as you practice PFC. (If you have many deposits, you don't need to do your allocations every day. Like Mike suggests in *Profit First*, "We are going to get you into a twice-a-month rhythm shortly that will make this process manageable."

6. Let's celebrate what you just accomplished. Although the 1% profit you allocated to your profit account is small, you now have become profitable. The reason you can say that is because you took that money, put it into a separate account and you're not going to touch it. If you commit to the process, take your profits first, and don't touch them, then your profits will be there at the end of the quarter. Congratulations.

Do this for every quarter and you are guaranteed to have a profit. This is a big deal, a huge deal. You have just separated yourself from most construction businesses out there. You should celebrate this. Now you probably shouldn't book a Caribbean cruise, but you should certainly celebrate this day with a cold one (tall glass of sweet tea or a beer, your choice.) If sweet tea or beer isn't your thing, then just tell me. I will celebrate for you.

I'm serious. You just became profitable. Celebrate in some small way and email me at shawn@profitfirstcontractor.com and tell me how you feel and what you did to celebrate.

Do not. I repeat, do not go out and buy another tool to celebrate. You have enough tools.

Week One: Cut Expenses

As discussed earlier in this chapter, we need to cut expenses in order to make this work.

Profit First Basics

> We have just accounted for at least 3 percent (1 percent in each of the PROFIT, OWNER'S COMP, and TAX accounts) of our income, so we need to cover that by cutting 3 percent from our expenses. To do that, I need you to print out two things:
>
> [1.] Your Expenses for the last twelve months.
>
> [2.]. Any recurring expenses: rent, subscriptions, Internet access, training, classes, magazines, etc.

"Expenses" in step one above are the items that make up this category from your P&L statement. You may want to look at your COGS and make sure you are getting every ounce of production out of your labor, materials, subs, and equipment as well.

> Now add up all the expenses and then multiply that number by 10 percent. You must cut costs by 10 percent. Now! No if, ands, or buts!
>
> So why cut by at least 10 percent, when we "only need 3 percent?" Because cutting costs doesn't mean the bills go away overnight. It may take a month or two to pay down balances owed on expenses we eliminate. More important, we need to start building cash reserves because by the start of the next quarter, we are going to move another 3 percent to your PROFIT, OWNER'S COMP, and TAX accounts, and then another 3 percent the quarter after that. So we will be accounting for that money quickly.
>
> You can easily find your first 10 percent in cuts by doing the

following:

> [1.] Cancel whatever you don't need to help your business run efficiently and keep your customers happy.
>
> [2.] Negotiate every remaining expense, except payroll.

This process can be made easier if you ask yourself (or with the other owners or managers in the company, or a spouse to get an outside perspective), "Do we really need this?"

Get serious about answering that question and trim the fat not the muscle. In order to operate more efficiently you may need to add some new expenses (bookkeeper, PFC coaching, or project manager). You aren't going to spend that money now, but you can start to plan for it as cash piles up, margins increase, and sale prices go up.

Before I started my coaching business, I was the chief operating officer for a trim and millwork company that employed twenty people. The company made zero profit, was heavily in debt, and the owner wasn't paying himself regularly. When we started turning the company around, the answer to the "Do we really need this" question was almost always "No." But then, after about a year and movement in the right direction, we would answer that question with "Not yet."

I tell you this story to encourage you and let you know it will get better. It's frustrating to always have to say "No," but PFC forces you to look at your business differently than you do today. The answer to that question will change to "Not yet." When you are thinking and planning effectively, you will be well on your way to running a mature construction business.

For more ways to cut expenses, refer to Chapter 7 in Mike's book, *Profit First*.

Twice a Month: The Tenth and Twenty-fifth

I wake up at 4:30am almost every day. Yes, I know that's crazy, but let me explain why. I have five kids and our house is a three-ring circus most days, especially the weekends. The stress of running my business meant that sometimes I didn't sleep very well, or I would wake up early in the morning and couldn't get back to sleep. On a few of those occasions where I couldn't get back to sleep I would get up and work.

I noticed something strange. Complete silence. That's a rarity in a house of seven people, especially when five of those people are wired for action, noise and destruction. The silence of those early morning hours is magical. I can focus on getting stuff done. I am super productive. Not only am I super productive, but I am exhausted by 8pm. I can't stay awake if I wanted to.

This was a problem at first because my body wasn't used to that schedule. But something interesting started to happen. I started to develop a rhythm to my day. Every day was focused. I would work on certain tasks in the early morning hours, get the kids ready for school during the regular morning hours, business work during business hours, family time after work, and then I would have to go to bed. 4:30am comes quickly if you stay up too late.

Eventually, this rhythm became a habit, and now it's a discipline. I actually enjoy it.

Establishing a rhythm for your business will have the same effect. You will become less reactive to issues and more focused on being proactive. PFC uses the 10/25 rule for establishing this kind of rhythm for your business.
Instead of checking the bank balance every time a bill comes in to see if you can pay it now or have to let it pile up with the others in the stack, you will process your allocations twice a month.
Transfer money from the income account on the 10th and 25th of the month. Pay the bills that are due for that time period. This creates a rhythm. This creates a habit. You will be less reactionary and more purposeful and focused.

Here's how Mike recommends getting started in *Profit First*:

1. Deposit all revenue into your INCOME account.

2. Every tenth and twenty-fifth day of the month, transfer the total deposits from the prior two weeks to each of your "small plate" accounts based on your [PTRs] and add it to any money (if any) that is already in there.

3. Transfer the full account balances for both your TAX and PROFIT accounts to the respective accounts at your second (no-temptation) bank.

See Mike's *Profit First* Chapter 3 on the why we set up no temptation accounts. These accounts make it more difficult to slip back into bad habits. Mike gets us started with his first three steps, but for PFC, you still have a little more work to do!

The next step in getting started with the PFC system is paying yourself - the owner.

4. Pay yourself out of the owner's comp account. Put yourself on a regular salary equal to the day one PTR. At times the amount in the owner's comp account may be more than what you pull out, depending on the income during that time period. That's ok. Let that money accumulate. You may need it if the income for a two-week period dips. That way you can keep paying yourself your established salary. If there's money in the owner's comp account at the end of the quarter or the year, then you can give yourself a raise. And that's essentially what the 1% increases each month will do.

If you're thinking you can't live on these numbers, then you are correct. That's exactly what PFC will show you, and you'll have absolute clarity on what you need to change. The pain, yes it sucks, will motivate you to change.

5. Pay your bills from the OPEX account. If there's not enough money in there, this is a sign to start cutting. But since you are

starting off slow, with just one percent here and there, you should be able to weather this storm.

Mike describes this step as "the Wake Up Call."

> When you don't have enough money to pay your bills, it is your business screaming at the top of its lungs, warning you that you can't afford the bills you are incurring. Or if there isn't enough money to pay your salary adequately, it is your business shouting out that you can't run your business the way you have been running it; otherwise you will continually compromise yourself. Implementing Profit First didn't cause the crisis—it just helped you notice there is one. You are spending more money than your business can support. But don't panic. By using [CPTRs], you will adjust to the tenth and twenty-fifth rhythm as comfortably as possible. Even if you can't pay everything on those dates, you must get into this rhythm because it will allow you to get a sense of the accumulation and flow of money. As a heart pumps blood rhythmically, forming a heart-beat, the lifeblood of your business, money should flow in a similar rhythm, not in a random, panicky pump here and there whenever you have funds.

Quarter One

The end of the quarter is here. It is time for a quarterly distribution. You have received thousands, if not tens or hundreds of thousands (in some cases millions) of dollars in revenue. You have been pulling profits out every couple of weeks, paying yourself, paying your bills, and watching the money accumulate in your various accounts. Now you are in the big leagues. You are going to take your first quarterly profit distribution.

Profit First Basics

The profit distribution is an award to the equity owners (you and anyone who invested in the business with money or sweat) for having the courage and risk tolerance to start the business. Don't confuse the profit distribution with Owner's Comp, which is pay for working in the business. Profit is a reward for owning the business. Just as you get a profit distribution when you own shares in a public company, for which you didn't do squat work-wise, so you get a piece of the profit from your own company. Profit is a reward for equity owners, and Owner's Comp is the pay for people who are owner operators in the business.

On the first day of each new quarter (or the first business day afterward), you will take a profit distribution. Remember, the Profit account serves a few purposes.

[1.] Monetary reward for the equity owners of the business.

[2.] A metric to measure growth.

[3.] Cash reserve for emergencies.

Tally the total amount of profit in the account (don't add any quarterly distribution percentages from deposits you received this day, yet) and take 50 percent of the money as profit. The other 50 percent remains in the account, as a reserve...

You will now take a distribution every quarter, just as you would from a large public company. These companies announce their quarterly income and then distribute a portion of the profits to shareholders. And that's exactly what you are going to do. Quarterly is a great rhythm, by the way. It is a long enough time between distributions that you start looking forward to them, anticipating them. But it isn't so frequent that they come to feel like a normal part of your personal income.

We will talk about how to plan for the long-term growth of your construction business, measure the metrics you need, and other things you need to do on a quarterly basis in Chapter 10. But for now, these are the marching orders and they match those in *Profit First*:

> Every quarter, you will take 50 percent of what is in the profit account and leave the other 50 percent alone…If your company has multiple owners, the distributed profit is divided up based on the percentage owned by each equity owner [according to the partnership agreement].*

*Partnership agreement? What do you mean you don't have one of those? You now a have profitable company. You better get a formal, legal document in place because if you want these profits to continue, you and your partners better get on the same page. The reason this hasn't been an issue before is because you've never made a profit. Once actual money enters the situation, then true intentions and desires are revealed.

Profit First Basics

> The profit distribution can never go back to the company. You can't use a fancy term like reinvest, plowback, or profit retention. No term you use will cover up the fact that you are stealing from your business. Your business needs to run off the money it generates in its operating expenses. The plowback of profit means you aren't operating efficiently enough to run off the operating expenses. And if you give the profit back, you won't experience the very important reward of your company serving you. You'll stay trapped in the Craftsman Cycle. So always take your profit, every quarter, and use it for your own purposes. It's celebration time!
>
> When you take your profit distribution, the money is to be used only for one purpose: for your personal benefit. Profit is intended to be your reward for having the guts to invest in your own business. Use it for whatever gives you personal joy. Maybe you go out for a nice dinner with your family. Maybe you feel joy in building up a fortress of money in your retirement fund.

But you're probably thinking about buying that tool you had to eliminate from the expenses. Well, it's your money, but I am guessing that this money, this actual profit, feels a bit different. It should. You worked hard to make and keep it. Congrats. Now enjoy it.

Pay Your Taxes

Until now, paying your taxes has been a burden. But with PFC, paying taxes is a result of making a profit (c'mon, every cloud has a silver lining, right?).

Profit First Basics

> Every quarter, you will also pay your quarterly tax estimates. Your accountant will probably give you estimates of how much you owe in taxes each quarter; this is when you pay them. You will actually reduce some of the pain you feel when paying estimates because on this very same day each quarter, you also will take that profit for yourself, above and beyond your salary.

Small Steps

I didn't plan on waking up at 4:30am every day. It was forced on me by stress and unhealthy living. But once I saw the benefits of structuring my day, being focused, and establishing a rhythm, then I was able to transform reaction into a habit. My crazy morning routine (contrast shower, drink 36 oz. of mineral infused water, Bulletproof Coffee, mediation, prayer, and journaling) started with one small step. No. It wasn't setting my alarm, that's the second step (and I don't use a regular alarm. I use a sleep cycle app to wake me up at the optimal time according to my circadian rhythms. I told you it was crazy). I realized the key to success to my morning routine was going to bed by 10pm the night before. If I committed to that small step, then it would set me up for success the next day.

The same thing applies to making PFC a successful routine for your construction business. Each quarter you need to evaluate your CPTRs and adjust them closer to your optimal PTRs. You may not know what your optimal PTRs are right now (that's why we use the recommend PTRs and the rules of thumb), but you will eventually find the sweet spot. The key to adjusting the PTRs is never to take a step back. You will see long term success if you slowly approach your recommended PTRs with small steps, rather than taking leaps toward them only to be forced to step back next month.

Both Mike and I recommend adjusting your profit, tax, and owner's comp PTRs by 1% each quarter.

Mike says, "If you can adjust further, go for it, by all means. Just remember, you can't 'undo your percentages' because that will undermine this new habit you have established. And don't forget, at the start of the next quarter, you will be doing this all over again."

Emergency Fund

Life happens. Markets change. Banks close. Recessions happen. Emergencies arise. You need a stash of cash to get your business through these emergencies. Here's how Mike describes how to create your emergency fund in *Profit First*:

> As your profits accumulate in your PROFIT account, and you only take 50 percent as a profit distribution, the remainder will act as a rainy-day fund. You sort of become your own bank. This is a good thing, but too much cash on hand can be a liability (sadly, people like to sue deep pockets), and money should be invested, not allowed to sit and stagnate month after month and year after year. This is a simple analysis of what to do with your rainy-day fund. Remember a little while ago, when I mentioned the ideal three-month cash reserve for your business, the place where you have enough cash saved to operate your business unscathed for three months if all sales came to a screeching halt and not another penny came into the business? Well, the Profit account is where this reserve accumulates, just for that circumstance. If you see that the money in it is in excess of a three-month reserve, you know this is a good opportunity to put money back into the business, to make some appropriate capital investments that will bring a lot more growth and a lot more profit...

That's what it looks like to invest in something. You determine a dollar amount to invest and you calculate the ROI.

Profit First is a Way of Life

I lost twenty pounds after following the Whole30 plan. It wasn't a diet for me. It was a lifestyle change. I can't go back to eating the way I used to. I mean, I can, but I don't want to. Now that I know how food affects me and my health, I can't ignore the facts. Some foods are fuel and some foods are crap. This is how I view the food I eat - with clarity.

PFC gives you the same clarity for your construction business. "This income is fuel for my business' growth (profit), and my family's well-being (owner's comp), and my obligation to the government (taxes), and the day-to-day operations of my business (total OPEX)." You are looking through the polarized lenses of PFC, and your construction business will never be the same. Your life will never be the same.

In order for your life to change, you have to lock in this system for your personal finances as well. Mike goes into great detail in his book about how to implement the Profit First system for your personal finances as well. I will summarize his key points here because I completely agree with what he says. I don't think I need to add anything to what he has already written. (Read Chapter 10 of *Profit First* for more details about implementing the Profit First lifestyle.)

Summary of the Profit First Lifestyle:

1. Know your numbers. Add up all your monthly bills, plus all your annual bills and the debt you owe.

2. Freeze your debt. Stop borrowing money. Pay cash for all purchases going forward. More on the debt freeze in the next chapter.

3. Set up multiple accounts and automatic payments to these accounts. Your compensation is your personal income. Treat this income the same way you do for your business income. This personal income is 100% of your personal budget.

Develop the PTRs for your personal expenses, including retirement, savings, and even a rainy-day fund.

4. Create special accounts. Do you have a big purchase on the horizon? Set up an account to siphon off money from your income to pay for it. Just like we did with the day zero to day one allocations, start small with one or two percent. Increase the savings over time. You'll get there if you start small. The most important thing is to start.

5. Be frugal. Spend less than you make. Look for discounts. Cut back on unnecessary expenses and start piling up money.

Action Steps:

The band-aid is off and now it's time to let the wound heal. These action steps are designed to help make the process end well. You've done the number crunching. Now it's time to speak with your CPA and/or bookkeeper (or find one) about your Profit First for Contractors plan. And it's time to develop your PFC rollout plan.

1. **Speak with your CPA.** Explain to her that you need to get your P&L statement in order. Ask her to show you the tax savings, in actual dollars, that you can realize by taking an owner's draw. Explain to her that you need to account for any owner's draws in your budget. This may mean that she produces your GAAP P&L statement and balance sheet, but then she needs to produce a PFC P&L that shows the value of your compensation in the COGS and/or expenses. This secondary report will most likely happen outside of your accounting software. We don't want you to monkey around with that, but you do need to see where the actual money is. Get on the same page with your CPA, or find one that will help run your construction business the way you need it to run.

2. **Get a professional bookkeeper.** Bookkeepers are different from CPAs. Bookkeepers are responsible for tracking and reconciling every financial transaction in your business. CPAs help you limit your tax liability and file your tax payments. Your CPA might provide bookkeeping services. If this is the case, then great. If you can't afford a regular bookkeeping service

(weekly or monthly), then find a bookkeeper who will drop in on a quarterly basis and help clean things up. This is money well spent and will help you avoid sending bad data to the CPA.

3. **Put Profit First for Contractors into motion.** You have your accounts set up and hopefully transferred 1% of your income into your profit account. Set your day one PTRs and make your next allocations (on the 10th or 25th of the month) according to the day one PTRs.

4. **Remind yourself to allocate your income.** Set a reminder on your calendar for the 10th and 25th of each month to transfer money into your accounts. I set reminders on my Google Calendar for the entire year. These reminders pop-up every 10th and 25th at 9am. Two weeks will fly by. Having these appointments with my money helps keep me accountable.

5. **Develop a rollout plan.** Starting with your day one PTRs, add 1% to the profit, tax, and owner's comp PTRs for the next quarter. You will have to decrease the total OPEX PTR by the sum of the percentages you added to the other accounts. Set the PTRs for each of the account categories over the next 4, 6, or 8 quarters. This is your rollout plan. Start small and build momentum. After a couple quarters, you can increase the PTRs and update your rollout plan.

Chapter 9

DESTROYING DEBT

Debt is not your friend. It never will be. It really is that simple.

Profit First Basics

> The Profit First system...will keep your focus on a super healthy business, working in your sweet spot to produce goods and provide services for ideal clients. This laser focus will automatically keep your costs down, allowing you to pay off debt faster and eventually increase your profit percentage. The tweak is, when you distribute profits, 99 percent of the money goes to paying down debt. The remaining 1 percent goes toward rewarding yourself. This way, the debt gets hit just as aggressively, but you still strengthen your Profit First habit.
>
> If you wait to implement Profit First until after you pay down your debt, you are less likely to ever build the business efficiencies that will permanently eradicate your debt and create a perpetual profit stream. Start the habit now, and eventually that 99 percent will go toward building up your cash reserves and your own owner distribution.

I was working with a client in a major metropolitan area. His business was growing by leaps and bounds (or so he thought). I asked him a few simple questions about his construction business and his answers were alarming.

"So you're projecting that you will have revenues more than 50% over the previous year?"

"Yes. It's crazy right now."

"And you are in the field directing, if not performing, most of the work?"

"Yes. I spend about forty hours a week on the jobs, and another thirty or so doing everything else."

"Are you paying yourself a regular salary?"

"Yes."

"So you're on the payroll just like an employee?"

"Well, no. I take owner's draws. That's what my CPA told me I should do."

"Ok, we can fix that. Let me ask you, what's your biggest problem right now? The thing you are most worried about?"

"Well, in order to keep up with the demand, I need to hire more guys, which means I need another truck as well. But my CPA told me that I should buy the truck before the end of the year because it will cut down on my taxes."

"Ok. Do you have any money to buy the truck?"

Silence.

"Well, no. But I can get a loan for the truck. That's not the problem."

To which I replied, "Yes, it is. You don't have any money. You're not paying yourself now for all the jobs you perform in the business, and you're not charging your clients for the seventy plus hours you are working for them. Borrowing money for a truck may grow your top line, but you can't borrow your way to profitability."

Silence.

You can't borrow your way to profitability. As Mike says, "Profitability isn't an event; it's a habit." Sure, you can use financing as a tool when you have a proven system of generating profits. But don't be fooled that your money problems can be solved by acquiring debt. It will only scale up your problems.

DESTROYING DEBT 151

Eliminate your debt by paying it with 99% of your profits. This is the first step in eliminating your debt. The next step is to avoid going into debt in the first place. Eliminating debt at the same time as trying to avoid it will be difficult at first because you are going to have to break old habits and develop new ones.

Debt elimination is simple with PFC. Almost all profit (99%) distributions go to eliminating debt. You need that 1% to go to yourself, for your personal use. That 1% will start to train your mind in getting pleasure out of a painful situation. When you can reduce the pain, then you will start getting more pleasure out of saving than you do out of spending.

Debt Elimination Strategies

Mike gives an efficient and effective step-by-step process for debt elimination in Profit First, and I am going to summarize it for you here. (Please read Chapter 7 of *Profit First* to find strategies for working a debt elimination plan.)

1. Start reviewing your twelve-month rolling averages for your income and related numbers. Dollar amounts can be deceiving, so percentages are more accurate.

2. Initiate a debt freeze. Trim all the fat from the expenditures. Cancel services, subscriptions, and find less expensive ways to operate.

3. Build a leaner team. Evaluate your employees for their productivity and efficiency. Look for ways to streamline. Before you lay anyone off, make sure you are not cutting out the muscle. Remember Parkinson's Law. People will work to fill the time that they have, so give them less time to get a task done. One immediate way you can see increases in productivity is to simply communicate the schedule to your employees based on the way it was priced. Clearly communicating the goals and objectives to your employees is a key to getting leaner. Produce more work in less time.

4. Time for more cuts. Negotiate everything. Call every vendor, supplier, credit card company, bank…anything with recurring fees and ask for better terms. You'll never know if you don't ask.

5. Start a debt snowball. Dave Ramsey is famous for coining this phrase, and Mike includes this as part of the debt elimination strategy. Pay down the smallest debt first. Don't worry about the interest rates. As Dave says, "If you were really worried about interest rates and math, you never would have borrowed money in the first place." Ouch, that's true. Start with the smallest debt first and put all your debt elimination funds toward that and make minimum payments on the others. Once the smallest debt is paid down take that amount and add it to the minimum payment you are making on the next smallest debt and so on. A snowball picks up size and speed as it rolls down the hill.

Debt is the enemy of your business. It will destroy you. If you don't develop a plan for your cash before you have it, then you will find yourself in a constant fight to keep it.

The Best Form of Self-Defense

I love fighting. In fact, I get into fights at least three times a week. No, I am not some Batman-like vigilante that combs the streets at night in search of injustices to defend. I am a forty-something father of five that trains in the so-called "gentle art" of Brazilian Jiu-Jitsu (BJJ).

BJJ is known as the "gentle art" because of its focus on grappling techniques instead of strikes. Make no mistake about it. Grappling with a two hundred fifty-pound man is anything but gentle. It's not just the big guys that I have to worry about. During my years of training, I have been beaten-up, choked out, and otherwise submitted by just about every kind of person – male, female, young, old, small, and yes, the big guys, too.

Although I have learned many techniques that should protect me in a physical altercation, the single most important aspect of training BJJ is knowing how to avoid a fight in the first place.

As important as eliminating your debt is to the overall health of your construction business, avoiding the debt to begin with is more important. You won't have to defend against the threats debt imposes on your business if you know how to avoid the debt in the first place.

Debt Avoidance Strategies

The strategies listed below will help keep the cash flowing into your business. When cash is good, PFC is in place (PTRs), and you can see where the money is going (banks accounts), then you won't have to borrow money. You avoid the fight.

1. Reverse engineer your weekly leads. In the next chapter, I will go into detail about how to develop your closing rates and how to use these metrics to predict your production, but for now you need to make sure you're getting enough calls to hit your revenue goals.

    For example, if your revenue goal is $1,000,000 and your average project size is $25,000, then you would need to perform 40 projects per year to hit your revenue goal of $1,000,000.

    $1,000,000 / $25,000 average per project = 40 projects per year

    If you need to look at three projects in order to close one, then you need to look at 120 projects per year to hit your revenue numbers.

    If you need to look at 120 projects per year, then you need to look at about two projects per week.

    120 projects / 52 weeks = 2.3 leads per week

    If you aren't looking at two to three projects per week, then you will not hit your revenue goal.

    Hitting this weekly goal should provide the sales you need to reach your yearly revenue target. When you consistently hit your sales goals, then the cash should follow – no need to fight.

2. Charge for professional services. In Chapter 7, I discussed how contractors should charge for the professional planning services they provide. Running around town and giving away work for free is classic craftsman cycle behavior. If your clients

don't have a plan for their projects, and they ask you to perform these services, then you should charge them. When clients hire you to perform these planning and design services before you do any of the work, then it means they trust you. When you establish trust with your clients, then they will spend more money with you. Clients that trust you allow you to provide a higher level of service. Higher levels of service are more valuable. Charging for value means higher margins. Higher margins mean more cash. More cash means avoiding the fight.

3. Do not finance projects. You are not a bank. You should not be required to finance your clients' projects. Financing the project is the client's job. Your job is to put the work in place. Structure your billings such that you have a positive cash flow throughout the duration of the project. This means that you should require a sizeable deposit before you start any project and bill according to the progress of the project. This goes for commercial work, too. Discuss the payment schedule with the owner of the commercial project and make sure that you work out a payment schedule that doesn't require you to finance the project.[8]

   An easy way to remember this is *bill early; bill often*.

   Note: Some construction companies offer financing as part of their services. In these cases, the cost of financing is part of the overall cost of the project. That's not what I am talking about here.

   Maintaining a positive cash flow on each project will ensure cash flow for the business. If you have cash, you don't need to fight for money.

4. Build up cash reserves. Many construction business owners fear the next downturn, recession, or market correction. This fear is compounded when cash is tight and you are in debt.

---

[8] Depending on your state or location, there may be laws limiting the amount of the deposit you can take for a project. You need to be aware of any such laws, and I recommend charging the appropriate amount according to the governing laws of your area.

DESTROYING DEBT 155

One way to relieve this fear is to build up cash reserves. In Chapter 8, I recommended leaving 50% of your profits in the profit account each quarter for emergencies. After you have eliminated your debt and you have at least three months of operating expenses saved, then I recommend building up your emergency fund to six months of operating expenses. Why six months? Because the next zombie apocalypse is not going to happen overnight. Whenever the next correction happens, you'll see it coming. You will have time to adjust your operations, and you'll have six months of cash on hand to deal with the fallout. Cash reserves mean the zombies will eat other construction businesses alive. You won't have to fight them.

5. Plan for big purchases. Once you have your cash reserves built up, then you will have proven to yourself that building up large amounts of cash is possible. You can then apply that same mentality, and the same cash generating activities, toward your next big purchase. You'll discover that with the right plan, you won't need to borrow money. You just need time. Avoid the fight by planning ahead.

6. Rent before you own. I know you think that you are losing money every time you rent a piece of equipment. Plus, you like to own stuff. It feels better. I get that. But when you rent equipment and tools, you don't have to pay the ongoing costs of maintenance and storage. You don't have to insure it, and you don't have to think about how much money you are losing when it is just sitting there. The great thing about most rental companies is that they have all those costs rolled into the rental fee. All you have to do is determine the rental costs, mark it up, and sell it to your clients. When you factor in all of the costs of owning a piece of equipment, property, or other asset, you might be surprised at just how expensive it is. Avoid the lure of ownership through debt. If you don't pay for something in cash, then you don't really own it anyway. The bank does. Avoid this fight. See number 5 above.

7. Don't overpay the owner. Ok, things are about to get real. Let's talk about you, the business owner, and how much money you are pulling out of the business. If you need $120,000 to live your lifestyle, but your business only generates $250,000 in total revenue, then you might think that borrowing money for

the business is the only way to grow. The problem might not be the business. The problem might be that you are an overcompensated employee in the business. If you need $120,000 in total compensation, then I suggest the business needs to generate at least $800,000 in total revenue with a 10% net profit. In this scenario, the owner would receive 10% of the $800,000 ($80,000) in owner's pay and half of the net profits (0.5 x $80,000 = $40,000). That's $120,000 in total compensation. If your lifestyle requires a total compensation from the business higher than the business can afford, then you have two options. You either increase the revenue and margin of the business, or you cut your lifestyle. Ouch. I know that one hurt, but it's the truth. The funny thing about PFC is that you can apply the same system to your personal life as well. Before you borrow money for the business, make sure that you, the business owner, aren't a drain on the cash. That's like punching yourself in the face. Don't do it. Avoid the fight by making sure that you are compensated at a level that the business can support.

8. Trust but verify. I hope that you have other professionals working for you that you trust. You have subcontractors, suppliers, vendors, insurance agents, and a CPA that all work for you. You trust them because you pay each of them to perform services for you. Just because you trust them, doesn't mean that you shouldn't verify the value of their services each year.

Talk to your subcontractors about their prices and the quality of their work. Do you know how they price their work? Are there things that you can do to get a better price? When I say, "a better price," I don't necessarily mean a lower price. Your subs might be able to do additional services that can save you time. Verify you are getting the best value from your subs.

Renegotiate terms with your suppliers and vendors. Ask them for discounts when you pay early. Will they deliver your materials to your job site? Can they waive delivery fees on orders of a certain size? You won't know if you don't ask.

As much as you love your insurance agent, are you sure you are getting the best price? Are you getting the best service?

Are you sure you have the proper coverage for your growing construction business? The insurance industry is an extremely competitive industry. If you have had the same insurance agent for more than three years, I recommend that you shop your coverage. If your insurance agent wants to keep your business, then your agent should be willing to sell you on her value every year. I recommend reviewing your insurance coverage and your agent's service every year. As your construction business grows, your insurance needs will also change. Verify you have what you need going forward.

You might need a new CPA/bookkeeper. I already discussed the problems with CPAs in Chapter 8. Don't let your numbers be held hostage for another year. Talk with your CPA about the services you need and verify that you understand how they can make you money. If your CPA can't explain to you how she can make you money, then find a new one.

Trusting in other professionals to do good work allows you to focus the on cash-generating activities of your business. Verifying you are receiving the best service is not only your right as the business owner, but also your obligation as the person that is responsible for the livelihoods of others.

There is security in numbers. Develop a team of professionals that fight for you and you'll never have to throw a punch.

9. Make your plan public. I am not suggesting that you post your budget on social media. That would be crazy. I am suggesting that you share your plan for profits (a.k.a. "the budget") with others in or around your organization. Sharing this information will create accountability and provide you with feedback on your plan.

    In Chapter 11, I discuss the power of having an accountability partner and the benefits that come through group coaching. You can avoid the fight with debt when you have a gang of others that are pushing you toward your goals.

    Whether you decide to seek accountability outside of your organization or not, at a minimum, I suggest you share your budget with the people inside your organization. This doesn't mean that you disclose personal information like salaries or pay structures, and it doesn't mean that you have to share proprietary information like trades secrets or even your markup. But you should share the overall targeted goals for costs and margins with your people and how you plan on achieving these goals. When people know how you are keeping score, then they can help you develop the strategies to win the game. Trust me. Your employees think you are rich just because you own the company. They don't understand how tight the margins are. You need to show them the plan and teach them how their decisions affect the outcome.

Avoid the fight with debt by surrounding yourself with people that will have your back.

10. Use debit cards instead of credit cards. This is the simplest way to avoid the fight with debt. Using debit cards feels different than credit cards. When you use a debit card, you know you are spending actual money. Credit cards trick us into feeling like it's not real money. The pain of using the credit card doesn't show up for thirty days. Using a debit card, on the other hand, forces us to ask the question, "Is there money in the account?" The exclusive use of debit cards makes us very aware of our bank balance, and, as discussed throughout this book, bank balance accounting works within the PFC system.

Using debit cards instead of credit cards means that you don't have to fight debt because you never stepped in the ring in the first place.

Wrestle your debt into submission and make a commitment to never borrow money again. This is a fight that you can win, but it will take some training. Winning the fight against debt will require that you make a profit.

Profit First Basics

No matter how much debt you have, know there is a way out. More than that, know that you are not the first person to be there. Many people have recovered from dire financial situations, and the key to doing that is in your hands…

> Now, I want to stop right now and make a strong argument for choosing profitability even when you have debt. In fact, when you have debt, you need to be more profitable than ever. Some people say they can't be profitable until they are out of debt, but that's not true. The only way to get out of debt is by being profitable. Debt accumulates because you have more expenses than cash to pay for them, so you borrow. You get a loan, a line of credit, a stack of shiny plastic credit cards. And yet the only way to have more money than you are currently spending is to be profitable.

Action Steps:

1. Get focused on eliminating your debt. Go to www.profitfirstcontractor.com and download the PFC debt elimination mantra. This graphic will change regularly. Check back every time you think you need to borrow money. This resource is not to make you feel bad, but to give you pause in that moment of fear and stress. Read the mantra out loud five times, take a deep breath, and then don't borrow money.

2. Read Chapter 7 of Mike's book, *Profit First*. This chapter is all about debt elimination. Put these strategies into practice.

3. Avoid taking on new debt by employing the strategies listed in this chapter. Start with one and work your way up from there.

Plan a celebration when you use 99% of your profits to eliminate your smallest debt first, and you have 1% left. Plan a small celebration. I know. It will be very small, but you are making progress. Celebrate it. Then get back to work.

Chapter 10

MEASURE YOUR METRICS

There's a cliché in business management that states, "What gets measured gets done." Some attribute the origin of this phrase to the 20th century "father of modern management" Peter Drucker. But further digging reveals that this phrase might have originated as far back as the 16th century Renaissance astronomer, Rheticus, as "If you can measure it, you can manage it."[9]

Whether a result of modern business management best practices or Renaissance star gazing, the thought is the same - if it matters, then you have to measure it.

That's what I discussed with Kelly and Janice Stitzer, in a roundabout way, the first time I met them.

"What kind of numbers do you think we should be seeing for a typical roofing business," Janice asked me in an impromptu conversation we had in her office in Westminster, Colorado.

Janice had invited me to speak at a construction industry meetup she and her husband hosted in the summer of 2017.

I answered her question with a question. "Are you a typical roofing company?" She chuckled a bit and shot a glance to her husband, Kelly, as if to say, *"Do you want to answer that?"*

Kelly responded as his eyes surveyed the room we were standing in, "Well, no. I like to think that we are different type of roofing company."

---

[9] Cornell, M. (2018). What's your feed reading speed? - The Experiment-Driven Life Blog - Matthew Cornell. Programmer, Research Software Engineer, Think, Try, Learn. [online] Matthewcornell.org. Available at: http://www.matthewcornell.org/blog/2007/7/30/whats-your-feed-reading-speed.html [Accessed 18 Sep. 2018].

In order to fully understand Kelly's response to my question, you have to see the office where Kelly and Janice run CIG Construction. If you didn't know better, you would think that you were in the offices of a tech start-up or a high-end design firm. The office has a lot of glass and steel and uses open spaces to take advantage of the natural light that pours in the front of the office. I would classify the style of the office as modern and minimalistic. "Clean" and "organized" are two words that come to mind when you walk in the front door, but the word that best describes what these two have created is "beautiful."

"I agree," I replied to Kelly. "I can see that you are a different type of roofing company. So I would expect your numbers would be different, too."

Over the next several minutes I learned a lot about their business. I learned that Kelly was the driving force behind the production and operations of the business and Janice was in charge of everything else, and she was the visionary behind the brand. Kelly's happy place was on the roof and Janice's was in the office. Another thing I learned was their numbers were screwed up. Janice shared with me that although they were hitting net profits of 30%, they were struggling with keeping an appropriate amount of cash flow.

"Well, I can tell you that if you have 30% net profits, then you should find someone to buy your business because that is an extraordinary net profit. Investors will line up for a return like that. But since you don't have any cash, then there might be something off in the way you are measuring your net profit," I told them.

I explained to them that I see this scenario all the time. The net profit on the P&L is high, but the owner doesn't draw a regular salary, and she has no cash in the bank. This usually means that the owner is taking an owner's draw and the value of the work the owner is doing in the business isn't being accounted for in the price of the work that is sold to the customer.

Janice and I discussed the issues that are inherent in the insurance restoration industry and how to overcome them. A couple months later, Kelly and Janice hired me as their business coach, and we started developing a plan to measure the right metrics for their non-typical roofing business. After our first coaching session Janice realized that she couldn't let the insurance industry dictate what mattered in her roofing business. She and her husband Kelly had to take control of their business. When they determined what mattered to them, then they structured their business to achieve the metrics they needed.

Just because you measure something doesn't make it important or make it produce the results you want. You can measure all kinds of things in your construction business, none of which may get you the results you need. It's like trying to lose weight by stepping on the scale every morning. Sure, that gives you some information. "I'm up a couple pounds today. I should not have eaten the entire pizza last night," or "I'm down a few pounds. I can hit up the taco truck at lunch today." (I love a good taco truck.)

A measure quantifies a thing. A metric compares a measurement to the baseline or standard set for that measurement. Standing on the scale is a measurement of weight. Thinking, "Oh crap, I am twenty pounds over my fighting weight!" is a metric.

In order for metrics to be effective we need to identify the right ones for your business and then develop a system to measure those metrics. There are two kinds of measurements - lead and lag measurements.

In terms of your construction business, net profit is a lag measure. We have to sell our work, produce the work, and track the outcome of that work. After these actions take place, then what remains is net profit. Net profit, in a classical accounting sense, is a lag measure. It is the result or the end of a system or process.

Lead measures, by contrast, are the activities that take place near the beginning of a process that influence the lag measurement.

In keeping with our example above, net profits are the lag measure and total income could be the lead measure. Without $1,000,000 in total income, then it will be difficult to produce a net profit of $100,000. You have to have the income first (the lead) before you can get to the profit (the lag).

Lag measures and their associated metrics are easier to define. These metrics are the results we want - a 10% net profit at the end of the year or to hire two employees by the end of the month. These are lag measurements. Knowing where we are going is important but understanding exactly what we have to do (the leading activity) is more difficult to determine. The reason lead measurements might be more difficult to define is that there could be multiple things that influence the end result.

Defining the metrics that matter isn't that difficult.

"We want a 10% net profit by the end of the year."

"We need to produce, on average, ten projects a year at $100,000 to hit our sales goals."

"We need to complete this job in ten months."

These are all lag measurements.

Implementing PFC helps you reverse engineer your construction business by establishing the metrics that matter (PTRs), revealing the inefficiencies, and providing you with a plan to achieve the results you want by changing the things that lead to these results.

Results are what Janice and Kelly were looking for. They thought they were measuring the right things - sales volume and net profits. But after some coaching they realized the lag measure of net profit was mathematically incorrect. They weren't accounting for the value of the owners' draws in their operational expenditures. And they were focused on the wrong metrics - sales volume of the typical roofing company. But any product or service sold at the wrong price will put you smack dab in the middle of the craftsman cycle.

Once we corrected the math of the measurements, then we were able to adjust their pricing strategy and generate profits. We also defined the metrics of success for their unique business, not a typical roofing business.

After they completed my Profit First for Contractors coaching program, Janice wrote to me and updated me on their progress:

> In 10-months' time, armed with a new knowledge base, we have been able to slowly piece together new systems and new pricing. We are constantly analyzing our numbers. It's a work in process and takes patience. No longer are we shooting for the vanity of top line revenues with no basis. With the guidance of Profit First [for Contractors] the concentration now is on "Real Revenue" and improving profit margins. This had positively affected net profits. The goal is to define our own success and run our business as profitable as possible.

Within 10 months of implementing PFC, Janice and Kelly hired two full-time positions and one part-time administration position. These new hires took the pressure off of running the day-to-day operations of the business and allowed them to concentrate on the main goal of any business - making a profit.

Metrics that Matter

Mike says, "[F]ocusing solely on top line thinking (sales, sales, sales!) does not lead to profitability." If the work you have now isn't producing profits, then getting more of the same work or managing it in the same way won't solve the problem. More sales actually make you less money.

Profit First Basics

> Efficiency increases your profit margins, or the amount of money you earn as profit on each product or service you offer. Increased profit margins will boost your company's profits without the need for increased sales. And then, when you kick the selling machine back into gear…, profits will skyrocket. So the method is simple: achieve greater efficiency first, then sell more, then improve efficiencies even more and then sell even more. Over time, speed up the back and forth between efficiency and selling until the two happen simultaneously.

You must focus on efficiency and the metrics that lead to increased efficiencies and doing more with less. Remember, Parkinson's Law is your ally.

As the first step in determining the metrics that matter for your construction business, we need to first chip away at the expenses that are going to make sense for your PFC way of life.

Chip Away at Expenses

If you haven't already, you should print out a report of all of your expenses and go through each one, line by line, and ask yourself, "Do we really need this?" And I've seen your expense report. There are categories like miscellaneous expenses, office expense, meals and entertainment, and other expenses. These very broad categories should be eliminated. Take a close look at the transactions in these categories and come up with a specific category for them. No more miscellaneous crap in the pantry.

I am not saying that you shouldn't spend money on meals and entertainment, but those frequent stops at Subway really aren't business meals. According to the IRS' website, "You must have records to prove the business purpose (under the applicable test) and the amount of each expense, the date and place of the entertainment, and the business relationship of the persons entertained."[10]

Assign every expense to a specific category. If you really have to stretch your definition of a category to include one of these expenses, that's probably a good sign that you should eliminate it. So cut it out.

Next, take a look at the dollar amounts for each of the categories for the past twelve months. Pick on the little guys. For any line item expense under $100 for the month ask yourself, "Do I really need this?" If the answer is "No," then eliminate it. If the answer is "Yes, I need this," then ask yourself, "What would I do if I didn't have this, if this thing was not even an option?" This line of

---

[10] Irs.gov. (2018). *Topic No. 512 Business Entertainment Expenses | Internal Revenue Service.* [online] Available at: https://www.irs.gov/taxtopics/tc512 [Accessed 1 Oct. 2018].

questioning will help you to innovate - to do the same or more with less.

Repeat this process every month and you will see your expenses drop, margins increase, and you'll find the sweet spot for your total OPEX PTR. Every construction business is different, and expenses will vary from business to business, but evaluating your expenses every month and asking yourself these questions are the lead measures that will lead to more profits.

If the goal is to reduce the PTR of total OPEX from 88% to 78% over the next year, then the lag measure is "Reduce expenses by 10% of total revenue over the next twelve months." The lead measure will be "Review all expenses each month for twelve months, eliminate any unneeded expenses, and set a budget for the next month."

Performing this task will not be easy. Measuring it will be simple. You either did it or you didn't. You either checked the box twelve times or you didn't.

But chipping away at expenses is only one aspect of streamlining your construction business.

Increase Your Price

Earlier in this book, we discussed the owner's draws and how they don't show up on the P&L statement. For many construction business owners, especially the owner-operators, the value of the work they do operating the business never shows up on the books. If it doesn't show up as a COGS or an expense, then you never give your customers the chance to pay for it. You never sold it to them.

When you start charging your customers for the value of the service you provide to them, your price will go up. When your price goes up, then you will lose some customers. This is a great thing.

Before you throw this book across the room, let me explain why this is really good for your business.

Let's assume for the sake of this example that you perform an average of 100 jobs per year and each of those jobs are priced at

$1,000. That would produce a total revenue of $100,000 for the year. If you double your prices to $2,000 per project, you could afford to lose half, 50%, of your customers and still make the same revenue.

Now you will be doing 50% of the work (50 jobs per year instead of 100) and still making the same income. You have six months of the year to do whatever you want.

"But Shawn, if I double my prices I will lose customers."

Yes, I know that. You need to lose some customers because the ones you have aren't paying you enough to make a profit.

But here's the key. Even though you can afford to lose half of your customers, you won't. Most of your customers love you. They love the service and the quality you provide. They will pay whatever you charge because they trust you. They (the customers who love you) are only paying your price because that's what you sold them. If you sell them your value, then they would buy that too.

So raise your price to meet the value you provide. Charge them for the estimating, design work, planning, project management and the bookkeeping services you provide for them. They will pay for it, but you have to sell it to them.

Back to the example. You can afford to lose half of your customers when you double your prices, but you probably won't. Let's say that you lost 40% of your customers. That leaves you with 60 jobs per year at your new price of $2,000 per job. That's $120,000 of total revenue (60 jobs x $2,000). That's 20% more revenue and you still have 40% of your time available to serve these customers (you can do 100 jobs, but only have to do 60 jobs).

This is key. Don't miss this. This 40% of time is important. The only way customers will pay for a premium service is if they receive a premium experience. You need to spend part of the 40% of the time you just got back on the experience you provide to them.

What does this look like? It means that when you are finishing up the job on the last day, you swing by the florist and pick up a bouquet of flowers and a thank you card and you leave it on the kitchen island. When you bring in your professional photographer to shoot the after pictures, you tell them you have arranged for a family photo shoot for your customers as a way to say thanks.

It means you develop a pre-construction process that helps them develop the project budget before you are willing to sign a construction agreement with them. (More about this process in the chapter on group coaching).

There are dozens of ideas that I am sure you can come up with that can increase the level of service and enhance the experience you provide to your customers. Write these down and just start doing them. Charge your customers for the value you are providing. Don't worry about the competition. They aren't making any money. You don't want to be just like them.

One last thing about raising your prices. I speak with hundreds of construction business owners every year and many of them say the same thing, "We want to do high-end work." The best way to get high-end work is to charge high-end prices. The customers you want to work for, the ones that have great style, pay high-end prices for everything else. Why wouldn't they pay high-end prices for your service?

PFC will help you determine what your true value is, and when you develop a system to sell your value, you don't have to compete on your price.

Communicate the Numbers to Your People

In his book, *Ownership Thinking: How to End Entitlement and Create a Culture of Accountability, Purpose, and Profit*, Brad Hams states, "In the absence of information, people make stuff up." When you combine this fact with what we know about Parkinson's Law (work expands to fill the time allotted), what you often end up with is people working longer on the wrong stuff.

This misalignment of production and purpose is not intentional. Your managers and employees feel like they are doing the right stuff as fast as they can. Remember our cartoon pilot from Chapter 8 - lost but making great time?

Working through the initial assessment, ripping off the band-aid, and developing your target PTRs has given you new information, information and numbers which you can't ignore.

PFC will reveal exactly which aspects of your construction business you need to improve, and now it's time to disseminate this information to your people. Now, you may not share the PTRs or other proprietary and internal financial information with your employees, but you need to share the other numbers of your business with them. Everything in your business has a number. As discussed earlier, every result (lag measure) starts with an initial activity (lead measure).

For the construction business owner, one of the simplest ways to achieve a gain in efficiencies, and thereby increased margins, is to communicate the schedule to your employees. You spend hours estimating projects, determining the price, and then selling that price to your customers. Closing a sale and starting a new project can be an exciting time for you, but we get caught up in the excitement of the close, or we feel relief because we just landed another Paul. The craftsman cycle requires more Peters, Pauls, and Patricks because these guys aren't producing the profits we need.

During this excitement (or stress) we often forget to communicate the numbers to our employees.

If you want PFC to really propel your business to the next level and change the trajectory of your life, then you need to use PFC to communicate the numbers to your people. One of the best ways to do this is to communicate the schedule that your proposals require.

In order for you to make a profit on your job, the work has to be performed within a predetermined amount of time. Communicating this time is critical to running an efficient and profitable construction business. And I am not talking about an overall schedule like the fact that your current job should take eight months to complete.

If this is the level of detail your people have, then Parkinson's law will kick in and your project will absolutely take eight months to complete (if not more).

You need to break the schedule down to its smallest unit and communicate these units to your people. You have a goal to complete a project in eight months, because that's what you sold to the customer. Your people need to know the numbers of those eight months. Where do you need to be seven months from now? Six months from now? Five months from now? Four months from now? Three months from now? Two months from now? What activities should be completed by next month, next week, and tomorrow to achieve the schedule that the project requires.

Remember, every proposal is a mini P&L statement. In order to achieve the total revenue with the net profits you set, you have to consistently be able to hit your numbers between those two goal posts. That means you have to be accurate with your COGS and expenses. Usually the biggest part of the COGS is the labor, and labor is essentially time.

Your people need to know the time you have allotted to perform the scope of work. They need to know the time for every line item in the scope of work. That's why I recommend holding a weekly schedule meeting with your people. If you want to improve your numbers, work more efficiently, and get faster results, you need to meet with your people every week for thirty minutes and work through the weekly schedule.

Here's a five-step process I have designed to clearly communicate the schedule to employees:

Step 1.   Review the previous week's schedule. Did we meet the goals for the previous week? If not, what do we need to do this week to get back on track? Make those adjustments.

Step 2.   With the corrections in place, what do you we need to do to meet this week's schedule? Set the goals for this week.

Step 3.   Set the schedule for next week. Now that we have discussed the changes that came up, made adjustments to get back on track, we can set the schedule for the next week.

Step 4.   Look ahead to the coming weeks and discuss what's coming up.

Step 5.   Repeat the process every week.

This scheduling procedure can be summarized like this: look back, look now, look ahead.

If you follow this process every week, and I mean every week, then your people will not only have the information they need to know to win the game, but also you will be able to fight against Parkinson's Law. Work will not be allowed to expand to fill the available time because time will be limited to the amount of work required to complete the task in a profitable way.

Everything in your business has a number. Make sure your people know the numbers. They want to win the game; they just need to know how to keep score.

Communicate the labor budget for every project to your people. Hold weekly scheduling meetings to disseminate the information and delegate the responsibilities of the project. Hold frequent huddle meetings to update the project status.

This level of communication will require more time, but as Steven Covey writes in *7 Habits of Highly Effective People*, "most people spend too much time on what is urgent and not enough time on what is important," and "the main thing is to keep the main thing the main thing." Focus your time on communicating the numbers to your people and they will have the information they need to make decisions. No more making stuff up and no more expanding work to fill time.

Implementing PFC and developing PTRs gives you the numbers. Now go share these numbers with your people. They are starving for information.

Track Your Sales

You've heard the expression, "What came first? The chicken or the egg?" This is a question that has been debated since the first century A.D. I don't want to get into a philosophical or religious debate because that would do us no good. I want to discuss reality. And if I want scrambled eggs for breakfast, then I better find someone who has a chicken and will sell me their eggs.

You may be like me when it comes to reading (or listening to) a book. Once you start, you just plow through the thing. I think it has to do with my ENTJ (it's a Myers-Briggs thing). I like to check off the boxes and get stuff done.

If you are plowing through this book without stopping to perform the initial assessment, dig into the numbers, and do the action steps in each chapter, well, then that's ok. That's what I did the first time I read Mike's *Profit First*, so I can't blame you.

But let me warn of you a potential pitfall I hear all the time from construction business owners who are caught in the craftsman cycle: "I need to get the system in place and perfected before I can implement it." Do not make this mistake. Perfection of PFC is not the solution to your problems. Starting PFC is.

PFC is designed so you can start slowly and build momentum. That's why it's called the initial assessment, not the final outcome. Someone once said, "Perfection is the enemy of good enough."

Selling more work and increasing top line revenue is not the solution to your problem. Selling your work at the right price *and* maximizing your margins through operational changes by implementing PFC is the solution to your problems.

One symptom of being caught in the craftsman cycle is telling yourself, "I will work on this thing when I slow down." This is not the mentality of a successful business owner. You are in business. You don't want business to slow down. Increasing your top line sales without changing the operational aspects of your business will keep you trapped in the craftsman cycle. But slowing down the sales until you have a fully designed PFC system will also not help you either. You need to keep the engine going.

You need to keep pushing in the sales department. Don't worry. Raising your prices and charging for the full value of your work will weed out the bad customers and help you focus on the right customers. As you keep adjusting your prices up, you will start to hear, "No, thank you." This is a good thing. You will start to identify your sweet spots. The sweet spots are the projects that make you the highest margins for the least amount of effort.

In order to find those sweet spots, you will need to test out your pricing and your sales techniques. You need practice. You need data, and you need to track this sales data in order to keep the pipeline full. Everything starts with sales. If you don't have sales, you don't have a business. You can have the best operations in the world, but without sales you can't make a profit. Your business starts with sales.

Top line revenue may seem like the ultimate lead measure. But what is one system's lead measure, could be the lag measure for the system that precedes it.

Let me explain.

Selling is where the money starts to come into the business. Without income (lead) we cannot have profit (lag). But before we have income, we must do something to close the deal. So, closing sales leads to generating income (lag).

PFC leverages human nature, bank balance accounting, and simplifies the process of managing your cash flow. PFC also identifies the areas in your business that need an operational overhaul in order to make the numbers work. PFC uses PTRs to manage the income of the business. Every dollar of income is categorized as such and then allocated to its predetermined role (PTR) within the business (profit, tax, owner's comp, total OPEX) twice a month.

But the income is a result of selling. Where income is the lead measure for the PFC system, income is the lag measure for your sales system. We have worked the numbers from income to net profit and made improvements along the way, but we should also work back from income to sales in order to understand how the engine works.

PFC is the engine that get us where we want to go, and sales is the fuel the engine requires. Understanding how to get the fuel from the pump into the engine is the final metric that we will discuss here.

Closing Rate

When I am interviewing potential clients for one of my coaching programs, a question I always ask is, "What's your closing rate?" A common answer from many struggling construction business owners is, "We get most of the jobs we look at."

I then ask them to give me a number, a percentage, of how many jobs they get versus how many they look at. Most business owners give me a percentage greater than 50%. I am not surprised by this because a high closing rate indicates an artificially low price point which leads to very little profits.

Higher closing rates are counterintuitive to most folks.

Don't you want more customers buying from you? Doesn't that mean you are a good sales person, if you have a high closing rate?

In my experience, profitable construction companies have a closing rate between 30% and 50%. Above 50%, the construction business will only be profitable if they specialize in one or two core services, and they have a streamlined sales process.

You will see this kind of closing rate for service contractors like plumbers, electricians, and HVAC companies because they offer convenience over price. The hot water heater is out, and mamma needs to take a shower. I am going to call a plumber to come out and fix the problem. I have an idea what it will cost, but in the end, I am not going to shop around. Mamma needs a hot shower. Just get out here and fix that dang thing.

Specialized service combined with a streamlined sales process will increase your closing rate. For service-based companies, the sale process is pretty straightforward. You pay us X amount of dollars just to show up and then we will diagnose the problem and let you know how much it will be to fix it. If you don't agree to pay the minimum service fee, then we don't come out.

Tracking your closing rate will inform not only your sale process, but also, you will be able to predict the sales volume of your construction business. When you can accurately predict the sales volume (income) of your business, then you'll be able to customize the PFC system to predict the future. It will be like having your own crystal ball.

CLOSING RATE is a sales ratio of closed sales to total sales calls. This metric can be measured in both quantity of sales calls and value of sales calls. (See the Appendix for a sample spreadsheet to track both).

Quantity Closing Rate

When you raise your prices, then you will start to hear some "Noes" from your potential customers. That's ok because you are going to start saying "No" as well. The number of noes and yeses is important information. If you can tell how many noes you have to hear before you get to a yes, then you can use this simple ratio to inform your marketing efforts and determine where your time is spent most effectively in generating business.

Calculating the quantity closing rate is simple. You divide the number of awarded projects by the total number of potential projects (and multiply by 100% to get it into a percentage). You may not consider all potential projects in this ratio. Let's face it. You are going to have crazy people call and want you to give them a price for their projects. They will describe a $500,000 project and have a $50,000 budget. These people have issues and will waste as much of your time as you let them. It is impossible to work for a prospect like this, so don't include them in your quantity closing rate. Including crazy people into your quantity closing rate will keep it artificially low, and we don't want that. You want to know, in general, how many potential projects you need to look at in order to make the total revenue.

For example, do you have to look at 100 jobs per year in order to close 35? This would be a 35% quantity closing rate. That's about two potential project calls per week. If you are getting four calls per week (assuming these calls aren't from crazy people as defined above), then guess what? You're going to be overbooked if you don't expand your operations.

The quantity closing rate is a great lead measure to predict your net profit. If you're getting less than one call per week, then you will know you need to ramp up some marketing efforts. Knowing your quantity closing rate will also help you establish your average price per project, which leads to the other type of closing rate you should track.

Value Closing Rate

Where the quantity closing rate is a good predictor of marketing efforts, the value closing rate is a great predictor of your production rate. The value closing rate is a ratio of the dollar value of awarded projects divided by the total value of all potential projects (multiplied by 100% to express it as a percentage).

The value closing rate will tell you the value of the work you need to look at in order produce your total revenue. For example, if your value closing rate is 33%, and your budget is based on $1,000,000 of total revenue, then you know that you have to look at $3,000,000 worth of work in order to hit your total revenue goal.

The value closing rate will also establish your average price per project. Using the numbers above, if you look at $3,000,000 worth of work and close on $1,000,000 worth of work and your average price per project is $150,000, then you know you will need to produce about seven projects per year in order to hit the $1,000,000 total revenue number. If you get a lead on a $50,000 project, then you will know this is way below your average project size and you may need to say "No" in order to stay in your sweet spot.

Another way you can use the value closing rate is to pre-qualify your potential customers. For example, if you get a lead on an estimated $500,000 project and the potential customer only has a $100,000, then you can't do the project (unless you want to go out of business). But this will inform you that even though the prospect doesn't have the budget for the project she described, you are getting calls for that type of project. This is great news. You're known for those types of projects. You just need to tweak your message to fit the ideal customer - the customer that has the right budget for the type of projects within your sweet spot.

Tracking your closing rates allows you to watch sales trends and adjust your marketing efforts as needed and prepare your production capabilities months before actual production is required. You'll be able to hire field personnel or office staff well ahead of the production rush, say "no" to the wrong type of customers and projects, and stay focused on the projects that will enable you to hit your numbers.

Incorporating these high-level metrics (meaning those numbers that give you a bird's eye view of your business without getting into the nitty gritty details) with your PFC system of cash management will reduce the stress that guessing creates. You can look at the hard data of your closing rates, even if this data is general in nature, and make the decisions that will drive the profitability of your business in less time with less effort.

I will end this chapter where we began, in Colorado, with CIG construction. At the time of writing this edition of the book, CIG Construction was recently featured in a web series produced by Fine Homebuilding called *Why I Build*. The video tells the story of Kelly Stitzer, how he got started in the construction business, and how he and Janice are changing the face of the roofing industry. I am not going to say that implementing PFC had anything to do with Kelly being featured by this national publication, but I am not surprised that when Fine Homebuilding went looking for excellent construction businesses to feature, they found CIG Construction.

When you know what to measure, things get done and good stuff happens.

Action Steps:

1. **Increase your price.** How would you answer this question: If your total revenue were $1,000,000 would you rather work for ten clients with the average price per project of $100,000 or one client on a $1,000,000 project? My guess is that you chose the latter. When you raise your prices, you will hear some "Noes." That's ok. The "Yeses" will be far more valuable.

2. **Communicate more with your people.** Hold a weekly schedule meeting, tell your people exactly what the production schedule is, and give them the pertinent information they will need to win the game.

3. **Calculate your closing rates.** Use the table in the Appendix or download the .xls file from www.profitfirstcontractor.com and start tracking your quantity and value closing rates. It will take some time to build up the data for these tables, so be patient. Revisit these closing rates after the first three months of tracking this data. After that, review your closing rates each month.

Chapter 11

GROUP COACHING

The worst enemy of Profit First for Contractors is not the market, your employees, or your customers. Mike explains, "The worst enemy of Profit First is *you.* The system is simple, but you have to have the discipline to implement it consistently, and that's where most of us fall short." We won't cut back on our tool budget or get rid of that vehicle that is weighing us down in debt. We believe the prescribed (yet false) industry standards, and this hampers our ability to innovate.

Mike elaborates, "[W]e *will* steal from ourselves, taking money we originally allocated for profit to pay bills. We will steal from our TAX account to pay our own salaries. We'll borrow. We'll beg… And when we let *Profit First* fall apart, what is the single biggest reason why? We go it alone."

I have a buddy, Scott. Scott and I played rugby together at the University of Tennessee. Scott and I didn't have a lot in common. He was athletic. I was not. He played on the A-side. I played on the B-side. Scott was a very good student (Electrical Engineering). I was average at best (Civil Engineering). Scott could end a fight. I could talk my way out of them.

The one thing we did have in common was our level of dedication. If we said we were going to do something, we did it. I think we both noticed this trait in each other within a few weeks of playing rugby together. Scott wouldn't stop - chasing down his opposite across the pitch to make the tackle during a match, running sprints in practice, and leaving everything he had on the pitch during every game. He was one of those quiet leaders. The kind who doesn't have to say much because he led by example. I respected that about him.

Years later, as my rugby career wore down (much like my knees), I turned to the gym to keep me in shape. I am not sure if I asked Scott, if he asked me, or if we both just found ourselves at the gym at the same time, but we became workout partners. I also don't remember (I'm getting older. Give me a break) if we ever discussed an official start time, but it was 5:30am.

Most of those early mornings would start with one of us arriving before the other, and when this happened the one who arrived first would sit on a couch in the lobby of the gym awaiting the arrival of the other. If your butt wasn't on the couch by 5:45am, then the tardy, or sometimes absent person would owe the other a dollar. That was our deal.

I remember one particular morning when I showed up first and started watching the clock. As the minutes ticked by, I thought, "Ha. Scott is going to owe me a dollar." With two minutes to spare, Scott walked in the gym and sauntered over to the couch. He wasn't wearing his normal workout attire. He was in what appeared to be the clothes he slept in and wearing his flip flops.

After he grabbed his customary cup of black coffee, he plopped down next to me with a smirk that told me, "You ain't getting my dollar."

I asked him if he was ready to get started, to which he replied, "Hell no. Not today. I am worn out." I asked him, "Then why are you here?"

He said, "I'm here for you. That's the way it works, right?"

I just nodded my head and said, "Ok. Let's go."

Years later, as our lives went in different directions, and our schedules changed, we eventually stopped being workout partners, but we remained close friends.

Then one day in the spring of 2003, I received a call from Scott. He told me that he was going to run the Chicago marathon. He invited me to train with him. I had no desire to run a marathon. At the time I was short and stocky (this was before Whole30) and my body was designed to lift heavy objects, not run long distances, but I thought, "Well this is something new. I'll give it try."

I agreed to train with Scott and he sent me the training schedule. We applied the same dollar rule to our training runs and started training. After one particularly hard run, hard for me, not hard for Scott, I told him, "I don't think I am the best training partner for you. I can't keep up."

Without looking up from his hamstring stretch, he said, "You're the perfect training partner, because I know that you will do what you say you will do. On the mornings that I don't feel like running, I know that you are in the parking lot waiting on me, and that gives me the motivation to get up and get my run in."

From a guy who doesn't say much, that meant a lot to me. After a few seconds of contemplation, I replied, "That's crap. You just don't want to owe me a dollar. You're motivated by spite."

Scott looked up and said, "Yeah, you're probably right. But spite is good motivation."

Whether Scott and I were competing in the weight room or helping each other maintain the proper pace during our training runs, we had partnered up to meet our goals. The benefits of having an accountability partner or group are many. Here are just some of the benefits you will get from seeking and establishing accountability with an individual or group:

1. You are committed to someone else. You gave your word and you don't want to be the person who doesn't follow through on your commitments. Plus, a bit of competition amongst friends is a good thing.

2. The pain of a process can be shared and therefore the pain can be diminished. A "we're all in this together" kind of attitude helps during those painful moments.

3. The process of developing a plan with feedback from others enables you to adjust the plan to stay on target when things don't go perfectly.

4. Meeting with a partner or group establishes a rhythm. A rhythm leads to a habit, and the right habits turn into disciplines over time.

5. You realize you're not alone. Without a partner or a group of people you can share your struggles with, you can feel isolated, alone, and like you are doing something wrong. An outside perspective can give you some relief that you aren't experiencing anything that others haven't experienced as well. The feeling of isolation and fear goes away, and your confidence increases when you know you have support.

PFC works, and an accountability partner or group will ensure you achieve your goals and will help you break down the big aspirational goals into smaller achievable milestones (flossing one tooth).

In this chapter, I will share with you the biggest mistakes Mike and I have found that people make when implementing Profit First for Contractors and how you can avoid them.

Mistake #1

Going it alone. You can make PFC work for your construction business, but doing it all by yourself will require the discipline to establish good habits and break bad ones. That's why getting help is a crucial first step. Don't go at it alone. Get an accountability partner or get involved in a PFC Group (more about that at the end of this chapter.)

Mistake #2

Too much too soon. By now you are fired up to start setting aside 10% profit, doubling your prices, paying yourself the salary you should have been paying yourself all this time, and slashing your expenditures. Whoa there cowboy! Hold on. I am glad you're fired up, but we need to stretch out, warm up, and then we can start to run.

If you start to pull 10% PTR out of your current income without becoming more efficient, establishing the right pricing strategy and adjusting your estimating and sale process, then you'll run out of money very quickly from your total OPEX account and you'll have to pull the money back out of the profit account. This defeats the purpose of the whole system. You must allocate profit and not or discounted equipment (or resources, or services) rather than sacrifice efficiency for what you think are savings."

Mistake #5

Stop "investing" in your company. This may sound shocking, but what many construction business owners consider investing is really stealing. Don't kid yourself. The reason you invest this money is because the actual cash doesn't exist.

Truly investing in your company means that you allocate a certain amount of capital in the company, calculate the ROI, and work a plan to realize that rate of return. Simply taking your compensation through owner's distributions is not investing. It's stealing. As discussed in chapter 2 , you'll never realize a true net profit in your company if you don't determine your COGS and mark them up by enough to pay for your expenses and pay for your net profit.

Mike adds, "When you find yourself in a situation where you feel the need to 'plow back' your profits, *stop* to reassess. There is always a better, more sustainable way to maintain the health of your business. You need to invest thought, not reinvest money."

Mistake #6

Dipping into the tax account. The first few tax cycles after implementing PFC might cause you to get into a bind when it comes to paying your taxes. Your CPA should have provided you with your quarterly estimated tax payments. When you allocate your income to your tax account according to your tax PTR, you may exceed the estimated quarterly tax amount your CPA gave you. As the amount in your tax account grows, you may be tempted to think, "I won't owe that much. I can pay some bills with that money. I can always make it up on the next allocation."

Wrong! Listen to what Mike says about "raiding the tax account."

Profit First Basics

> As your profitability grows, your taxes will, too. In fact, paying more taxes is an indicator that your business health is improving. Now, I am not saying you should ever pay more taxes than you need to (tax is just an expense like any other), but do realize that your taxes will grow as your business health does. So don't steal from your Tax account thinking you won't need that money for taxes. You will.

Read more about practical strategies to deal with saving for your taxes while you're paying off debt within this system in Chapter 11 of *Profit First*.

Mistake #7

Profit First for Contractors is simple, but some people make it more complex. Have you ever heard of Occam's razor? The term Occam's razor refers to the philosophical idea or scientific principle that of any given set of explanations for an event occurring, it is that the simplest one is the correct one.

PFC is simple. PFC should not be complicated. That $10,000 check you just received is not really $10,000. Some portion is for your profit, taxes, owner's comp, and total OPEX. Figure out your PTRs and allocate that check according to your PFC plan. Simple. Done. Now do it for every check you receive. Don't make it more complicated.

Mike says it best: "Don't try to outsmart the system. Just get comfortable with the fact that sometimes getting the results you want is way easier to achieve than all the hard work you have put in to get the results you don't want."

This sounds odd, but it's true.

Mistake #8

Skipping the bank accounts. The PFC system works because it is an actual machine for managing your actual cash. This machine exists at your bank(s) in the form of multiple accounts. You can see it at work every time you log into your bank. The machine will be staring you in the face.

Some construction business owners try to do PFC in a spreadsheet without setting up the bank accounts. Spreadsheets are fine for tracking information, but you need the information in real time at the point at which you are making the decision. This is our natural behavior. "Do I have enough money for this? I need to check the bank account." That's what we do. In the moment, it is so difficult to say, "Do I have enough money for this? I better reconcile the spreadsheet, evaluate my situation, and then make the decision." Too late. You'll end up looking at the number in the one bank account and guessing that you'll be okay.

PFC is a physical system that you must set up at your bank to help you enhance your natural behavior of bank balance accounting. If this machine only exists in a conceptual format, then you'll never be able to realize its full potential.

Allowing PFC to exist only in a spreadsheet without the actual bank accounts set up is like trying to tell a homeowner that her project is complete when the drawings are finished. Crazy, right? You have to physically build the foundation, frame the walls, put the roof on, and so on. You don't have a house until you put all the pieces in place. The same thing applies to PFC. You can't skip the bank accounts and make the system work.

Group Coaching and Personal Accountability

You now have all the information you need in order to implement PFC for your construction business, and while you can certainly do this yourself and avoid the mistakes listed above, both Mike and I recommend finding a certified Profit First Professional (PFP) to support your efforts. Having an experienced PFP expert to coach you through the hard times can make all the difference. PFPs are there, waiting to help you succeed.

I never would have been able to complete a marathon without Scott. The task was too big and the training too long. But we came up with a simple plan. And I'm not even talking about the six-month training regiment we downloaded from the internet. I am talking about the simple and effective accountability system we set up. If you don't show up on time for the training run, you owe the other person a dollar. That's all it took for Scott and me to get started, and that simple dollar system created the accountability we needed to ensure that we showed up and did the work.

Owning a construction business is hard enough in and of itself. I want to make it easier for you to get the results you are looking for. That's why I developed the Profit First for Contractors Legacy Platform.

The PFC Legacy Platform, located at www.ProfitFirstContractor.com, provides you with all the resources you need to successfully implement PFC for your construction business. At the time of writing this first edition of PFC, the PFC Legacy Platform provides you with additional resources and support you can use to successfully implement PFC in your construction business.

Here's what you will find in the PFC Legacy Platform:

1. Free resources with additional training and support for implementing PFC in your construction business.

2. An online course that teaches you much more than just the PFC system (See the website for pricing for this online course). This online course will teach you strategies and tactics for the following areas of your business:
    - Time management
    - Sale techniques - my signature Paid for Planning program
    - Estimating and budgeting techniques
    - Financial reporting and planning
    - Scheduling
    - Communication systems
    - Organization for your construction company
    - Contract and documentation controls
    - Hiring and recruiting policies and procedures
    - Mission statement creation and vision casting for your construction business
    - Much more!

3. PFC group coaching. Once you have signed up for the online course, you are eligible to enroll in PFC group coaching. You

can take your PFC system to the next level by learning from other construction business owners in a group setting. The group coaching sessions will meet each month and cover a specific topic within PFC and the online course. You'll be able to learn from others and see what is working and what is not. You will be asked to share your experiences with your PFC group, and you will receive help from others. As part of the group coaching program, you will also have access to a private PFC community forum where you can interact with other construction business owners and managers to get the support you need to run the race. Once you are a member of the PFC group coaching program, you never lose access to the content of the online program or the private community. That's yours forever (unless you're a jerk in the community, then I will kick you out.)

4. Once you have completed the online course and the group coaching, if you want to work with me and my team personally, then we can design a mentoring program for you. Mentoring programs are a minimum of six months, and we take a deep dive into all aspects of your business and work together to get you the results you need to take your business where you want it to go.

Accountability and coaching will help accelerate your success in PFC. I have designed these programs to help you in every way possible. Use the free resources to get started making the profit you need in your business and gain some traction. Sign up for the online course to go deeper in solving the problems you have in your business. Join a PFC group to learn from and share with others, or work with me personally to scale up your success and maximize your profits.

I am on a mission to change the way the world views the trades. The best way to do this is to help as many construction business owners as possible run world-class businesses. I believe if I can do this, then the next generation will realize the value of the trades and consider a career in the construction industry as a worthwhile, lifelong pursuit.

When I read Mike's *Profit First* for the first time, I had an epiphany. "I need to take this system and this message to the construction industry. This can save businesses and change lives." So that's what I did. I became a Profit First evangelist. I spent a year going through the PFP certification process and started teaching the system to my coaching clients as part of my coaching services.

Every time I worked with a client in implementing Profit First, the same questions and challenges came up. I realized that I needed to translate the Profit First system into terms that would relate specifically to construction business owners to further simplify the system. That translation is what you are reading now - *Profit First for Contractors*. All the Profit First concepts are the same, but I have created certain terms and adjusted a few methods of Profit First to specifically help construction business owners.

My hope for you is that you will join me in my mission to change the way the world views the trades. Running a world-class, profitable construction business is the first step in achieving that goal.

Will you join me?

Action Steps:

1. Check out the free resources at www.profitfirstcontractor.com and check out the online course, group coaching, or contact me about the mentoring program.

2. Take your profits first.

Epilogue

Imagine, if you will, a small elementary school. Just outside the back door of this small elementary school is a playground. And just beyond the playground, is a busy highway. Now imagine you are a teacher at this school. You are responsible for the safety and well-being of the students in your care.

Each day at recess, you are supposed to let the children go outside and play on the playground. But you're afraid that the children, being children, are not aware of the dangers associated with getting too close to the busy highway. Each day, as recess approaches, you start to feel anxious about releasing the children. In fact, playtime won't really be *play time*. You will have to monitor the activities and location of each child to make sure they don't get run over.

Can you imagine this? Can you see the school building, the playground, the busy highway, and can you see the look of fear on your face each time the bell rings for recess? That's a pretty frightful scene.

Now I want you to imagine that one day you show up to school and someone erected a fence around the playground. This fence is solid. This fence is durable. This fence could take a hit from a Mack truck and still stay intact.

On this day, you know you can release the children at recess and you don't have to worry about where the children go. You don't have to worry about what the children do. Not only are the children safe, but you are also able to enjoy watching the children do what they do. Play.

Can you see this picture? Can you feel the relief that the fence provides? That's a drastically different picture from the first scenario, isn't it?

What you realize is that with the proper fence, or boundary, in place, you have a lot of freedom. You don't have to worry about keeping the children close to you. You can let them roam and play and do what children do. All you have to do is focus on maintaining the fence. Establishing the right boundary creates freedom for you.

Many construction business owners are like the teacher in this example. They have these businesses they are responsible for. And much like children, each business wants to run free. That's exactly what the business will do. It will run all over the place and eventually get run over as it drifts into oncoming traffic.

Maybe this has happened to you. You got hit with a huge tax bill at the end of the year. SPLAT! You have never been able to pay yourself for all the time you work in your business. SPLAT! You ran out of money and needed to go into debt just to pay your bills. SPLAT! You've been busy for months, but you have no money to show for it. SPLAT!

What you need is a sturdy fence, a boundary to define the area of your playground. If you had boundaries, then you could have the freedom to do what you need to do as long as you stay within the established boundaries.

It sounds counterintuitive, but there is freedom through boundaries. We don't like boundaries because they seem restrictive, but the opposite is true. PFC creates the boundaries for your construction business. With the boundaries that the PTRs create (profit, tax, owner's comp, and total OPEX), you can focus on doing the work that you enjoy without the fear of getting run over. When you add in the benefits of additional support through the PFC Legacy Platform and group coaching or mentoring, then you will develop the ability to maintain the fence. Maintaining the boundaries that lead to operating a profitable construction business requires much less effort and energy than having no boundaries at all.

Free yourself from the fear of running your construction business. Use PFC to erect your boundaries. Get help in maintaining these boundaries through accountability and you'll be like the teacher who looks forward to showing up for work every day.

*I read a lot of books. The playground example came from one of the books I read and has always stuck with me. Unfortunately, I do not remember where I read it. By the time this edition went to print, I had not been able to locate the original source. My apologies to the author, but I promise that when I find you, I will give you full credit for this wonderful example. If you know where this example comes from, please email me at shawn@profitfirstcontractor.com. I'll send you a token of my appreciation.

Acknowledgments

I finished writing the first draft of this book almost two years to the day after I left my job as the COO of a trim and millwork company. I left that job because life is too short to have regrets.

My wife has an incurable autoimmune disease. It is slowly and painfully destroying her body, but you would never know it if you met her. She is the most joyful person I know, and her constant encouragement of my stupid ideas is a daily inspiration.

As her health declined, we decided that we needed to live life in a different way - to celebrate every day we have together. Some days are better than others. The bad days are bad, but they make the good days incredible.

This book is for you, Katie. You pick me up when I am low. You knock me off my high-horse when I think, "I'm all that." And you encouraged me to go fly fishing that night in Wyoming. Those hours of peace and solace were the genesis of this book. I thank God for your only flaw – bad taste in men. I love you.

This book is for my five children. You can't do anything you want. You read that right. You can't do anything you want, but you can do everything you focus your time and attention on. You will be forced to live the Profit First lifestyle while you are under my roof, so that when you have your own roofs, you will be free. I love each of you with my whole heart, but remember our family mantra – mamma first.

This book is for my mentors. First and foremost, I want to thank Richie Norton. You inspired me, educated me, guided me, and supported me on this journey. My stupid idea turned out to be the smartest thing I could ever do. I am eternally grateful for you.

Next, Dustin Kaehr. Who knew that day we met in New Mexico at the 4-H livestock yard, speaking to a crowd of four would be the start of a very special friendship? I am grateful for your guidance not only on how to start writing a book, but also on how to finish one. I am a better leader, husband, father, and friend because of knowing you.

Last but not least, I want to thank Mike Michalowicz. Mike's passion for inspiring entrepreneurs to be better, live better, and create better businesses is contagious. Thank you for allowing me to take your system, make it my own, and change the lives of construction business owners everywhere. You inspire me to do more with the gifts God has given me.

This book is for my clients. Thank you for trusting me with your hard earned money. Thank you for showing up, doing the work, and changing your mindset. I wouldn't have been able to write this book without your stories, your feedback, your struggles, and your victories. I was only able to share some of your stories here, but your stories inspire me to learn more, teach more, speak more, and give back more to you and this industry. Thank you for your support.

Thank you to the team behind the scenes that made this book a reality. Thanks to Kelsey Ayres, Mike's assistant, for answering my never-ending questions. You are a saint. Thank you to Meggan Robinson for sculpting the trash I first sent you into something that could then be edited, and then revising it again into something someone would actually want to read. You are a warrior. Thank you to Liz Dobrinska for taking my call the day before Thanksgiving and helping me turn the content of this book into a visual masterpiece online. You are an artist. And thanks to my assistant, Kristie Cormany. When you started, I told you, "I've never written a book before. This will probably be painful for both of us." It was, but I am grateful for your thoroughness.

This book is for my friend, Tim Roman. I will never forget how you encouraged me when I was questioning whether I should go "all-in" on this book deal – "I bet the house every time I walk out the f*ing door." You're the man.

Finally, this book is for the construction business owners that are up early every day, working their tails off for their families and their communities, with little respect for what they do and how they do it. I hope this books serves you and helps you escape the craftsman cycle. The world needs you. Your work is important.

APPENDICIES

Appendix 1

PFC GLOSSARY OF TERMS

PRICE: the amount of revenue generated by selling work, or the money your clients pay for your product or service. Interchangeable with revenue and income.

COSTS: the money the business owner pays to purchase labor, materials, subcontractor services, and equipment (also known as Cost of Goods Sold - COGS).

MARKUP FACTOR: the number, when multiplied by the COGS, that is used to determine the price. Typically shown as "1+MARKUP."

MARKUP: the amount of money that you add to your COGS to determine your price, usually expressed as a percent.

EXPENSES: the overhead costs the business requires to operate. This money is not tied to a particular project or direct cost. If it's not a COGS, then it's an expense.

NET PROFIT: the amount of money remaining after the COGS and expenses are subtracted from the total revenue.

COST OF GOODS SOLD (COGS): the money a construction business spends on labor, materials, subcontractors, and equipment. This is what a construction business buys, marks up, and sells to its customers.

LABOR: the cost of paying the employees of a construction business a wage or salary. This is a COGS. This is not labor (wages or salaries) in the expense category.

MATERIALS: the cost of purchasing the items a construction business sells to customers (building materials, fixtures, permits, etc.). This is a COGS.

SUBCONTRACTORS: the cost of hiring independent contractors (non-employees) to perform a service which may include installation of materials. This is a COGS.

EQUIPMENT: the cost of the necessary machinery, apparatus, or gear required to perform a job or install materials. This is a COGS.

GAAP: Generally Accepted Accounting Principles. These are the rules your CPA follows.

INCOME: the amount of money the business generates or receives for the work it produces. Interchangeable with price and revenue.

REVENUE: the amount of money the business generates or receives for the work it produces. Interchangeable with price and income.

TOP LINE REVENUE: the total income or sales a business receives or generates by selling a product or service. This term also refers to the location of this number on a profit and loss statement - at the top of the report.

GROSS REVENUE: the total income or revenue or sales produced by a business before any deductions.

P&L: an abbreviation for Profit and Loss Statement

BALANCE SHEET: a statement of the financial position of a business, which states the assets, liabilities, and owner's equity at a particular point in time.

OWNER'S DRAW: the money distributed to the owner(s) from the retained earnings of the business.

MARGIN: the difference between the cost of a product or service and its price, usually expressed as a percentage of the ratio of gross profit to price.

PERCENTAGE OF TOTAL REVENUE (PTR): the ratio of a given dollar amount to the total revenue. The PTRs in PFC are the allocation percentages for your PFC bank accounts - income, profit, tax, owncomp, total OPEX.

GROSS PROFIT: the difference between the price and the COGS, usually expressed in dollars. The dollar amount remaining to pay for the business' expenses and have a net profit left over.

GROSS MARGIN: the ratio of the gross profit to the total revenue, expressed as a percentage. The percentage remaining to pay for the business' expenses and net profit.

EXPENDITURES: a PFC term that means the total amount of COGS and expenses. Used in the PFC formula:
INCOME - NET PROFITS = EXPENDITURES

REAL REVENUE: the difference between the income a business receives and the dollars that go to subcontractors and materials. The actual cash a business manages.

Target Allocation Percentages (TAPs): a *Profit First* term used to describe an ideal percentage of "real revenue" that gets allocated to your bank accounts.

OPERATING EXPENDITURES: the amount of money left over to operate the business after all other expenditures have been funded. The total revenue minus the costs of the materials, subcontractors, the dollars of net profit, owner's compensation, and tax.

TOTAL OPEX: total operating expenditures. A PFC term that is the operating expenditures plus materials and subcontractors.

CLOSING RATE: a sales ratio of closed sales to total sales calls

SPLAT: the sound of your business getting run over. Erect a sturdy fence to avoid this sound.

Appendix 2

MARGIN & MARKUP TABLE

Use this table regularly.

MARKUP FACTOR	MARGIN %
1.15	13.04%
1.20	16.67%
1.25	20.00%
1.30	23.08%
1.35	25.93%
1.40	28.57%
1.45	31.03%
1.50	33.33%
1.67	40.12%
1.83	45.36%
2.00	50.00%
2.25	55.56%
2.50	60.00%

(Page intentionally left blank.)

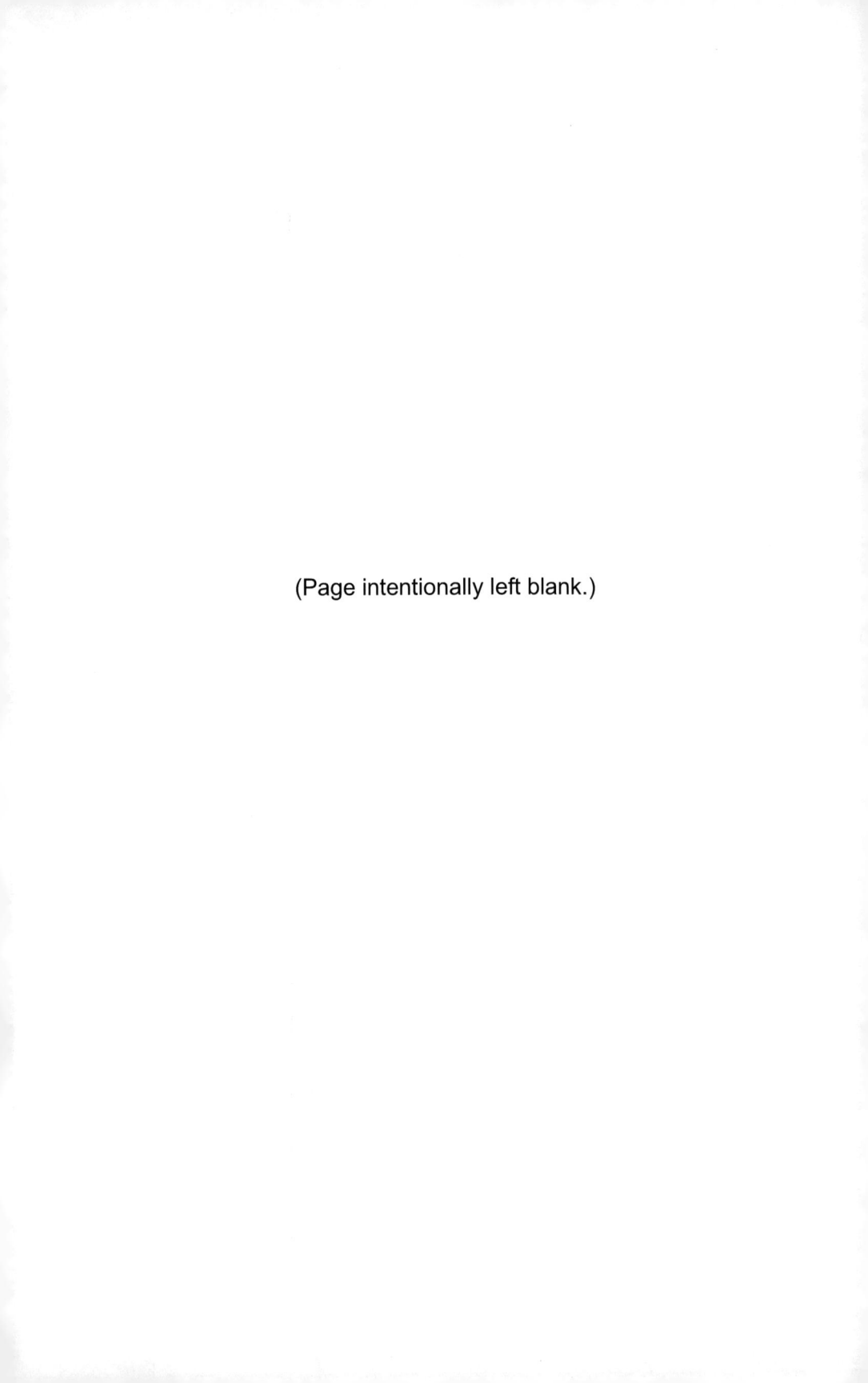

Appendix 3

PFC INITIAL ASSESSMENT FORM

(See the following page for the **PFC Initial Assessment Form**)

208 PROFIT FIRST FOR CONTRACTORS

	ACTUAL	TAP of REAL REVENUE	PF$ of REAL REVENUE	DELTA	FIX	PFC ACTUAL PTR (% of TOTAL REVENUE)	PFC RECOMMEND PTR (% of TOTAL REVENUE)
TOTAL REVENUE	B3						
MATERIALS & SUBS	B4					G4	H4
REAL REVENUE	B5	100%				100%	100%
NET PROFIT	B6	C6	D6	E6	F6	G6	H6
OWNER'S COMP	B7	C7	D7	E7	F7	G7	H7
TAX	B8	C8	D8	E8	F8	G8	H8
OPERATING EXPENDITURES	B9	C9	D9	E9	F9	G9	H9
TOTAL OPEX						G10	H10

PFC TRANSLATION

Appendix 4

CLOSING RATE TABLES

PROJECT IDENTIFIERS		QUANTITY	INCOME STREAMS				VALUE · $ of SALES CALLS		
		# of SALES CALLS	VALUE of PROPOSAL per INCOME STREAM						
PROJECT NUMBER	Project Name	Client	New Construciton	Renovation/ Remodel	Service & Maintenance	Special Projects	SUM of PROJECT INCOME STREAMS	RUNNING TOTAL	TOTAL AWARDED
A4	B4	C4	D4	E4	F4	G4	=SUM(D4:G4)	=H4	(Enter SUM of $ Awarded) on this line
A5	B5	C5	D5	E5	F5	G5	=SUM(D5:G5)	=I4+H5	(Enter SUM of $ Awarded) on this line
A6	B6	C6	D6	E6	F6	G6	=SUM(D6:G6)	=I5+H6	(Enter SUM of $ Awarded) on this line
A7	B7	C7	D7	E7	F7	G7	=SUM(D7:G7)	=I6+H7	(Enter SUM of $ Awarded) on this line
A8	B8	C8	D8	E8	F8	G8	=SUM(D8:G8)	=I7+H8	(Enter SUM of $ Awarded) on this line
A9	B9	C9	D9	E9	F9	G9	=SUM(D9:G9)	=I8+H9	(Enter SUM of $ Awarded) on this line
A10	B10	C10	D10	E10	F10	G10	=SUM(D10:G10)	=I9+H10	(Enter SUM of $ Awarded) on this line
A11	B11	C11	D11	E11	F11	G11	=SUM(D11:G11)	=I10+H11	(Enter SUM of $ Awarded) on this line
A12	B12	C12	D12	E12	F12	G12	=SUM(D12:G12)	=I11+H12	(Enter SUM of $ Awarded) on this line
A13	B13	C13	D13	E13	F13	G13	=SUM(D13:G13)	=I12+H13	(Enter SUM of $ Awarded) on this line
	TOTAL - ALL PROJECTS		=SUM(D4:D13)	=SUM(E4:E13)	=SUM(F4:F13)	=SUM(G4:G13)			=SUM(J4:J13)
CLOSING RATES		←— QUANTITY CLOSING RATE ——→	= # Awarded / Total # Per Income Stream	= # Awarded / Total # Per Income Stream	= # Awarded / Total # Per Income Stream	= # Awarded / Total # Per Income Stream	TOTALS PER INCOME STREAM		
BASED on # of PROJECTS	=(# of Projects Awarded) /(Total # of Sales Calls)		=D14/$J$13	=E14/$J$13	=F14/$J$13	=J14/$J$13			
BASED on $ of AWARDED	= I$ of Projects Awarded /(Total $ of Sales Calls)	←— VALUE CLOSING RATE ——→	= $ Awarded / Total $ Per Income Stream	= $ Awarded / Total $ Per Income Stream	= $ Awarded / Total $ Per Income Stream	= $ Awarded / Total $ Per Income Stream			

210 PROFIT FIRST FOR CONTRACTORS

PROJECT IDENTIFIERS		- QUANTITY - # of SALES CALLS	INCOME STREAMS — VALUE of PROPOSAL per INCOME STREAM				- VALUE - $ of SALES CALLS		
PROJECT NUMBER	Project Name	Client	New Construciton	Renovation/ Remodel	Service & Maintenance	Special Projects/ Commercial	SUM of PROJECT INCOME STREAMS	RUNNING TOTAL	TOTAL AWARDED
16-001	Smith Guest House	1	$450,000.00				**$450,000.00**	$450,000.00	$450,000.00
16-002	Jones Remodel	2		$67,345.34	$575.23		**$67,920.57**	$517,920.57	$575.23
16-003	Barkley Kitchen	3		$26,000.00	$4,236.45		**$30,236.45**	$548,157.02	
16-004	Finn's Diner	4				$12,000.00	**$12,000.00**	$560,157.02	
16-005	Matthews Repair	5		$15,312.23	$2,400.00		**$17,712.23**	$577,869.25	$2,400.00
16-006	Van Dyke Deck	6	$125,000.00				**$125,000.00**	$702,869.25	
16-007	O'Brien Int Repair	7			$159.23		**$159.23**	$703,028.48	$159.23
16-008	Reynolds - Master Bath	8		$55,000.00			**$55,000.00**	$758,028.48	$55,000.00
16-009	Vista Park Commons	9				$13,457.00	**$13,457.00**	$771,485.48	
16-010	Hodges - Ext Repair	10			$3,546.89		**$3,546.89**	$775,032.37	$3,546.89
	TOTAL - ALL PROJECTS		$575,000.00	$163,657.57	$10,917.80	$25,457.00			**$511,681.35**
			74.19%	21.12%	1.41%	3.28%	TOTALS PER INCOME STREAM		

CLOSING RATES									
BASED on # of PROJECTS	60.0%	<--- QUANTITY CLOSING RATE --->	50.0%	25.0%	80.0%	0.0%			
BASED on $ of AWARDED	66.0%	<--- VALUE CLOSING RATE --->	78.3%	33.6%	61.2%	0.0%			

www.ProfitFirstContractor.com

touch it, so you have to ensure that your business can handle the reduction in operating expenditures.

Start with small chunks and build up from there. Your rollout plan over the next four, six, or eight quarters might seem like a long time, but the next two years will fly by. Slow and steady progress toward your goals over the next year to two years will set you up for much bigger success in the long run. Two years is nothing compared to the next ten years.

Mistake #3

Growth for growth's sake. Edward Abbey once said, "Growth for the sake of growth is the ideology of the cancer cell." But this is what many construction business owners think is the path to success. "I have to grow the business. I need to do more work, add more services, hire more crews, get more subcontractors…" And the craftsman cycle continues. Construction business owners view building a successful business out of sequence. They try to grow the business and then figure out if what they are doing is profitable. Instead they should figure out what makes them a profit first and grow a business around that.

Slow growth is not sexy. It's not flying by the seat of your pants and faking it until you make it, and it's not about hustle and grind (don't even get me started on that). Slow growth is about doing things with a purpose, testing out ideas before you launch them, and using data to inform your business. Slow growth means that you will become a student of the game, tracking the money and deciding where it must go for your business to grow.

Everyone loves Chick-fil-A. Well probably not everyone, but I live in the South. We love our Chick-fil-A down here. Did you know that it took Chick-fil-A fifty-four years to reach one billion dollars in sales? Did you know that it only took them another seventeen years to reach over 9 billion dollars in sales? When you see Chick-fil-A now, you think "big, corporate franchise." But they are the perfect example of how slow growth leads to sustainable scalability. But it took them 71 years.

Your slow growth starts today. You can be profitable today when you set that profit aside, do not touch it, and change the way you operate your business.

The end of the month is coming up, or the end of the quarter. You are only a short time away from your first profitable month/quarter/year. I don't care how small your victory is right now. It is something and that is more than many construction business owners will ever accomplish.

Mistake #4

Not reviewing your expenses. I was recently speaking with a client of mine who was struggling with cash flow. (He liked PFC but had yet to implement it fully.) He said, "I don't understand why this seems to happen each month."

When I hear this statement, I cut to the chase. "Are you reviewing your expenses every month? I mean looking at every penny that is going out the door and asking yourself, "Do we really need that?" The answer to most cash flow problems starts with your expenses.

I remember reading an interview with Oprah years ago, before I started my first business. In the interview, she was asked about how she was able to achieve and maintain such a high level of success. She said that one thing she does to take control of what she can control is to sign her own checks. She knows every penny that is going out of her bank account.

You need that same level of awareness for your business. You may have a bookkeeper, office manager, CPA or other personnel that has responsibility or authority to pay the bills on your behalf. But you must review your expenses every month. When you review your expenses every month, you must cut any expenses that you don't need, but make sure not to cut the wrong things. Remember, you want to trim the fat, not cut out the muscle.

Mike says, "Money is made by efficiency—invest in it. If a purchase will bring up your bottom line and create significant efficiency, find ways to cut costs elsewhere, and consider different

Made in the USA
Columbia, SC
05 January 2019